D0404616

3⁹⁵

Simone Weil

AN INTRODUCTION TO HER THOUGHT

John Hellman

DISCARD

College of the Rockies
Library

FORTRESS PRESS   PHILADELPHIA

Copyright © 1982 by Wilfrid Laurier University Press
Foreword copyright © 1984 by Fortress Press

First Fortress Press paperback edition 1984

All rights reserved. No part of this publication may be reproduced, stored in a retrieval system, or transmitted in any form or by any means, electronic, mechanical, photocopying, recording, or otherwise, without the prior permission of the publisher, Fortress Press.

Library of Congress Cataloging in Publication Data

Hellman, John, 1940–
  Simone Weil: an introduction to her thought.

  Includes index.
  1. Weil, Simone, 1909–1943. I. Title.
B2430.W474H39 1984   194   83–48917
ISBN 0-8006-1763-0

K471C84   Printed in the United States of America   1–1763

CONTENTS

Foreword   v

Introduction   1

1. Simone Weil in Her Times   7

2. The Insufficiency of Politics   17
    A Brilliant Theoretical Insight   17
    What Marx Had Not Foreseen   25
    Factory Work   33

3. Patriotism and Hitler   37
    Is God French?   37
    On Patriotism: False and True   41
    Hitler, the New Caesar   43

4. History, the Old Testament, and Roman Tradition   47
    The Jehovah of the Bible versus the
        Father of the Gospels   47
    Rome: The "Great Beast of the Apocalypse"   52
    The Roman Tradition in Western History   55
    De-Romanizing Christianity   59
    The Cathars and Romantic Love   65

5. Religion   74
    Possession by Christ   74

Non-Christians and the Love of God   77
Nurses against the S.S.   80
The Unity of "Attention"   82
The Three Secret Presences of God   90

Conclusion   98

Appendix   104
The "New York Notebook" (1942)   104

Index   108

FOREWORD

SIMONE WEIL (1909–1943). Social thinker and activist, religious convert and spiritual writer known for her unusually altruistic life, Simone Weil was born into a wealthy, close-knit Parisian family in which she distinguished herself from childhood by an instinctive generosity and empathy for the less fortunate which would mark her entire life. Although physically frail and awkward, she quickly demonstrated a determination to share the lot of the working poor by joining them at the work place and giving what she had to them without counting the cost to her career or health. After demonstrating intellectual brilliance as a student of Alain, and as a *normalienne*, Weil became prominent in Parisian non-Stalinist Marxist circles for the strength of her commitment to the working class and the originality of her approach to social and political questions. She performed certain dangerous services for the Trotskyist movement, and her widely remarked-upon articles in *La Révolution prolétarienne* drew the attention of Leon Trotsky who, in an essay and then in a personal confrontation, denounced the unorthodox tendencies of the young woman's thought, which she defended without any concession. As a beginning *lycée* professor of philosophy at Le Puy she attracted some notoriety for her insistence in consorting with local stone breakers and a determined effort to get to know their working conditions and problems firsthand. Despite her appearance and health, she was accepted in the roughest working-class circles, and given the honor of carrying the red flag in the May Day parade of miners at St. Etienne.

Simone Weil's growing frustration with the lack of firsthand knowledge of workers' conditions among revolutionaries and union leaders impelled her to take leave of her academic career and work in several factories in the Paris region during 1934–35, and on a farm at Cher as well. The *Journal* of her factory experiences and her subsequent essays on the proletarian condition were original and incisive. They confirm her dissatisfaction with extant political theory and revolutionary or trade-union programs as well as her determination to share the lot of the poor and oppressed. She began to place her acts in accord with her ideas in a completely selfless way—to the somewhat horrified fascination of the Parisian left-wing intelligentsia. For example, when the Spanish Civil War broke out she immediately set out to join the anarchist-syndicalist forces stationed in Aragon, where she severely injured her leg in an accident. Her shock at the brutal treatment of humble and defenseless prisoners by certain Spanish revolutionary leaders furthered her dissatisfaction with revolutionary ideologists.

Simone Weil's disillusionment with the various spokespersons of the proletariat led her to conclude that only Charlie Chaplin and Jesus Christ truly understood the proletariat's condition. Her factory experience, she said, had killed her youth, and "the affliction of others entered into my flesh and my soul"; she had "received forever the mark of a slave, like the branding of the red-hot iron the Romans put on the forehead of their most despised slaves." In this state of mind, and while continuing to endure severe physical suffering, Weil visited a Portuguese fishing village on the festival of its patron saint. There she came to the realization that Christianity was preeminently the religion of slaves, that slaves could not help belonging to it, and so she had to join the others.

During 1937–38 Weil had several religious experiences centering on the person of Christ. At that time she began to fill notebooks with reflections and aphorisms on spiritual matters, which compare in power and originality with those of Blaise Pascal. Her first reaction to the rise of Adolf Hitler had been a militant pacifism but in March 1939, with the German invasion of Czechoslovakia, she abandoned this stance. At the end of that year she began to study the Bhagavad-Gita and Sanskrit, and soon began to formulate stimulating and original reflections on the differences between Eastern and Western cultures and values. This also led her to elaborate a distinctive exploration of the origins of Nazism and Fascism, which she saw rooted in the imperialistic and racist attitudes of the ancient Romans and Hebrews. At the beginning of 1940 she drew up a

"Memorandum on the Formation of a Front-line Nursing Squad," which is a concrete result of her effort to articulate a set of heroic values that antifascists could juxtapose to the warrior virtues trumpeted by both the Axis powers and French nationalists. She would continue her efforts to formulate a philosophy and political theory for the Resistance in London during the war, and to fill notebooks with reflections which have led some to claim that she was the greatest spiritual writer whom France produced in the first half of this century.

Her empathy for the hunger on the Continent inspired the fasting which weakened her resistance to tuberculosis and contributed to her tragic death in 1943.

INTRODUCTION

Simone Weil's remarkable life would have brought her renown even if she had never written a word. But, despite her frequent illnesses and early death at thirty-four years of age in 1943, and her lack of opportunity to formulate a major intellectual testament, she left some important intellectual achievements. Not only is she remembered as one of France's most prominent political thinkers of this century[1]—one of the most original and creative non-Stalinist Marxists of her generation[2]—but she also left religious and philosophical writings of great originality.

Albert Camus, who played an important role in publishing her works after the Second World War, was particularly taken with her early political thought and described her in 1951 as "the only great spirit of our time."[3] Camus, a lucid nonbeliever, has left few comments on her later, more religious writings, but although her views of Christianity were frequently described as heretical, and her differences with Roman Catholic doctrine were always sufficiently important so as to prevent her from joining the church, she became one of the three most important intellectual influences on Pope Paul VI[4]—

1 See, for example, Roy Pierce's *Contemporary French Political Thought* (London, 1966) which includes her as one of the six most important contemporary French political thinkers along with Raymond Aron, Albert Camus, Bertrand de Jouvenel, Emmanuel Mounier, and Jean-Paul Sartre.

2 For some of the extravagant praise which greeted her early writings see below, pages 17, 23.

3 In *L'Express*, February 11, 1961, cited in Pierce, *Political Thought*, 121.

4 Peter Hebblethwaite, *The Year of Three Popes* (London, 1978), 2. The other two, according to Hebblethwaite, were Pascal and Georges Bernanos.

one of the most learned and doctrinally orthodox of modern Popes. Despite the fact that she was later attacked for infidelity to her own Jewish tradition, a prominent contemporary French Jewish intellectual has described her as "the greatest spiritual writer which France has produced in the first half of this century."[5]

However original and brilliant her writings, Simone Weil's life was so out-of-the-ordinary, and so coincided with her own philosophy, that it is difficult to separate her life from her thought: "No one has more heroically put his acts in accord with his ideas."[6] Simone Weil's insights and analyses, however, have a power and originality of their own which need not be tied to her altruistic life to be recognized, and in some respects they can be appreciated with greater clarity if they are considered by themselves. Simone Weil died in broken health, having written letters but not a single book. Does this mean that her thought was incoherent or—left in fragments as it was—incomplete? An expert on her thought has written: "What amounts to a single world view, with both its paradoxes and its logic, does appear through her writings, even though she died before setting it out formally herself."[7] It is a major purpose of this work to set out this world view in a way which Simone Weil did not have the opportunity to do, and—without ignoring its paradoxes—to test its logic. Her thinking has far more logical underpinning to it than is at first apparent on reading her individual essays. An effort to disengage the key themes in Weil's writings can help us to examine the seeming contradictions and inconsistencies, grasp the background to several generalizations which seem rash in isolation, and, in general, clarify her thought. We may then better evaluate the claims for brilliance and originality made on her behalf.

Why must the structure of Simone Weil's thought be distilled, extracted from the corpus of her writings? One major reason why she never ordered her thoughts as they are in this book was that she almost always focussed her arguments toward her audience—and these varied from Trotskyist political militants and anarchist union leaders to monks and medievalists. And since much of her writing was correspondence of one sort or another and never intended for the general public, she sometimes adopted extreme positions in order to highlight, for purposes of dialogue, her differences with her correspon-

5 Wladimir Rabi, "Simone Weil entre le monde juif et le monde chrétien," Sens 7 (July 1979), 169.
6 Simone Pétrement, La Vie de Simone Weil, 2 vols. (Paris, 1973), 1: 10. Condensed and translated by Raymond Rosenthal as Simone Weil: A Life (New York, 1976).
7 David Raper, "Introduction" to Gateway to God (London, 1974), 21.

dent or particular audience. Thus she wrote her early—and most complete—essays on politics as a Marxist for her fellow Marxists. Therefore she could assume a basic appreciation for Marx's thought, and sympathy for his goals, among her readers and engage in a fraternal, "in-house" criticism of his insufficiencies. Her intention in this context was obviously to ameliorate Marxism, not reject it out of hand as a reading of her essays in isolation might imply. She was at the time a great admirer of Marx—but a vigilant and critical one who set high standards for Marxism and her fellow Marxists out of fidelity to the inspiration of the master himself.

This same attitude of critical fidelity which informed Weil's Marxism also characterized her later adherence to Christianity. Some of her essays from the latter period of her life, if read in isolation, make her out to be as much anti-Christian as Christian. But again it was her demanding lucidity and spiritual exigency which were behind the apparent severity of her views. An example was her "Letter to a Priest," which is often cited as her definitive, harsh critique of the Roman Catholic Church and the Old Testament. It was not written for the general public, but rather to set out in an extreme way what she saw as the barriers between her position and that of the church. It was sent to one of the several curés she met who could not grasp how a woman with her deep spirituality, with her love for the church, could continue to refuse its sacraments. And, on the other hand, her long essays in Need for Roots, despite the religious dimension so vital to their arguments, were written for the hard-minded leaders of the French Resistance, and so their spiritual aspects could not be articulated so explicitly as they might have been for someone who shared her deep religious convictions. Her remarkable essay on Attention, in contrast, was written for the Catholic students of Father Perrin, and she made this notion, which she first acquired from her teacher Alain, into a deeply religious concept despite the fact that one need not share religious belief to grasp it. And this is true of several of her most important ideas: although often framed for religious persons, they did not require religious belief to be appreciated, as Albert Camus, among others, demonstrated.

In sum, most of Simone Weil's writings were composed in a tone of fraternal correction toward groups or organizations for which she held deep affection at the time—Marxist revolutionaries, trade-unionists, Catholics, Resistance leaders—she saw no need to describe the commitment which inspired her effort. It would be as distorted to employ isolated remarks of Simone Weil against Marxism, Christianity, or the Resistance as it would be to use the words of the Prophets to undermine Israel.

Like her teacher Alain, Simone Weil went from one subject to another with an unorthodox, critical—often humorous—attitude and with little concern to pull the whole together. But she did not follow Alain's example in insisting that her own thought was essentially antipathetic to any systematic formulation. Thus when readers of Weil have perceived a single, highly original world view behind her disparate writings, they have been frustrated at their inability to find it expressed in a clear and coherent way. This is an important stimulus to this study.[8]

Previous books on Simone Weil have tended to centre on her piety and religious writings. Since she led an unusually worthy life, fact has influenced the exposition and conclusions. Most of her biographers have portrayed her as a sort of saint,[9] while a few others have seen her as an aberrant personality—sexually obsessed,[10] or psychologically disturbed.[11] One critic simply labelled her an esoteric

8 This author's experience in teaching her thought to undergraduate and graduate students has been particularly enlightening in this regard.

9 The best biography of Simone Weil is by her old school friend (and noted philosopher in her own right), Pétrement, Weil. A condensed English version of this work, replete with errors, has been published as Simone Weil: A Life, translated by Raymond Rosenthal (New York, 1976). For an interesting debate over Simone Weil see J. M. Cameron's admiring review article of this work in The New York Review of Books 24/3 (March 3, 1977), 3-7, and Conor Cruise O'Brien's subsequent reservations: "The Anti-Politics of Simone Weil," The New York Review of Books 24/8 (May 12, 1977), 23-28

The Pétrement work largely supercedes Jacques Cabaud's L'expérience vécue de Simone Weil (Paris, 1957), which was another thoroughly researched, admiring, but relatively balanced study.

Among the works which imply, or frankly assert, that Simone Weil might well have been, or was, a saint are P. Bugnion-Secretan, Simone Weil: Itinéraire politique et spirituel (Neuchâtel, 1954); Victor-Henri Debidour, Simone Weil ou la transparence (Paris, 1963); Bernard Halda, L'évolution spirituelle de Simone Weil (Paris, 1964); Marie-Magdeleine Davy, Simone Weil (Paris, 1966); Gaston Kempfner, La philosophie mystique de Simone Weil (Paris, 1960); J. M. Perrin and Gustave Thibon, Simone Weil telle que nous l'avons connue (Paris, 1967); and Maurice Schumann, La mort née de leur propre vie (Paris, 1974).

The two most important studies in English are also in this category: G. W. F. Tomlin, Simone Weil (London, 1954), and Richard Rees, Simone Weil, A Sketch for a Portrait (London, 1966).

10 Charles Moeller, Littérature du XXe siècle et Christianisme (Paris, 1963), 1: 240-49. This analysis is partially approved by Philippe Dujardin, Simone Weil: Idéologie et politique (Grenoble, 1975), 35-36.

11 Paul Giniewski, Simone Weil ou la haine de soi (Paris, 1978). On pages 267-69 Giniewski discusses others who, he feels, share this view.

cult figure without much talent.[12] Most such opinions seem influenced by the prejudices of the various authors against any individual deeply sympathetic to Catholic-Christian spirituality—and against any claim to "sainthood" in general.

Simone Weil did not write to gain recognition as a religious thinker. The thought of Simone Weil, in fact, profoundly unsettles many believers. Albert Camus demonstrated that an atheist appreciative of the humanistic values in the Judeo-Christian tradition can have far more sympathy for many of her themes than can guardians of religious orthodoxy.[13] Weil's ideas are not necessarily tied to the heroism or folly of her life; they should also be appreciated in their own right. Thus she urged that people worry less over how she lived, and why she said what she did, and be more concerned over whether what she said was true or not.[14]

This study does not argue that the thought of Simone Weil was inspired by the sorts of special graces God sends only to his saints—or by the special energies displayed only by unusually obsessed, deviant personalities. Rather it sets this issue aside as unrelated to an appreciation of her remarkable intellectual achievements. In any case the testimony of those among Simone Weil's biographers, relatives, and friends who knew her best suggest that Weil was neither the gloomy, suicidal, Cathar bent on self-destruction nor the austere, humourless

12 Cf. Henri Peyre, French Novelists of Today (London, 1967), 283. Professor Peyre lamented that "... her most erratic pronouncements on political or social thought ... have been published and naively pondered over," while "her influence on religious thinking, Catholic and Protestant, was doubtless second to none in the years 1948-1960 and is only now being assimilated and perhaps weakened."

13 Weil's good friend, Father Perrin, for example, has never ceased to warn of the headstrong and heretical tendencies in her thought, most recently in his contributions to the collective work, Simone Weil: philosophe, historienne et mystique, edited by Gilbert Kahn (Paris, 1978). For example, he commented that "... more than once, when a passage of scripture was bothersome or seemed difficult to accept, she fell back facilely on the hypothesis that certain words might have been added by the primitive community and did not come directly from Christ. She often seemed rather casual about the historical reality ..." (55).

Father Perrin helped inspire, and contributed to, a collective work of theologians, including the late Cardinal Jean Daniélou, S.J., which warned of certain tendencies in her thought. Cf. J. M. Perrin, Réponses aux questions de Simone Weil (Paris, 1964).

Professor Peyre remarks with some justice that Weil's thought "may well have acted more powerfully on agnostics than upon orthodox Christians, and some clerics ... have uncharitably denounced the dangers of her views" (Peyre, French Novelists, 284).

14 This sentiment was particularly strong in her last letters to her parents. Cf. Pétrement, Weil, 1: 9.

ascetic one might infer from some of her isolated writings. She was, rather, a mischievous, often playful individual, with a good sense of humour and that special sense of irony which seems to distinguish onetime students of the *Ecole Normale Supérieure.*

Despite the remarkable power of her religious writings, Simone Weil always remained something of the bright *normalienne:* she brought fresh and astute solutions to a host of spiritual problems; she thought about history, politics and modern scientific culture in a new and stimulating way. A broad look at Simone Weil will reveal a character at once more attractive and more human. This perception, in turn, will cast her work in a clearer light—important work that has been "heard of" but little studied in the English speaking world.

1

SIMONE WEIL IN
HER TIMES

Torn between the threats, or temptations, of Communism and fascism, the generation of 1930 in French intellectual life was unique in the gravity of the challenges they faced and the quality of their responses to those challenges. The young people who began to make their reputations early in that decade ranged from brilliant Communist writers such as Louis Aragon, André Malraux, and Paul Nizan to some of the brightest, lights of the European "fascist international": Robert Brasillach and Pierre Drieu la Rochelle. Simone Weil belonged to that generation and as an introduction to her view of the world it is useful to situate her within it.

She was, in many respects, an extremist in a generation given to extremes. It is particularly instructive to compare her form of extremism to that of her peer and contemporary, and only rival as the outstanding woman of her intellectual generation in France: Simone de Beauvoir. Although in many respects the two shared a common background, their reactions to them grew further and further apart through the years. While Simone de Beauvoir began with an extremely "spiritualist" orientation and evolved toward more and more political concerns, Weil, to Beauvoir's chagrin, moved from political commitment to religious preoccupations.

Simone Weil had much the same early intellectual formation as Simone de Beauvoir. Both of these women, like so many of their generation of French intellectuals, came from comfortable and rela-

7

tively cerebral upper middle class families. Simone de Beauvoir's provincial Catholic aristocratic family, however, was an early target for her scorn and rebellion, while Simone Weil's urbane, secular-Jewish family life called forth her undying devotion, despite all her hostility to the "bourgeois" society at large. Both Simone de Beauvoir and Simone Weil were prodigies in early revolt against the society in which they lived. But while a bitterness against a stultifying, narrow, hypocritical, and antihuman milieu ran through all Simone de Beauvoir's subsequent writings, Simone Weil's family life is reflected only in her emphasis on unconditional affection. Indeed, her deep attachment to her parents and brother influenced all her analyses of human relationships, their nobility and their limitations. Simone de Beauvoir, at first a "dutiful daughter," was soon a rebellious adolescent. Simone Weil, the precocious apple-of-her-parents' eye, was soon in rebellion against a brutal society—but not against the father, or the family, who meant so much to her.[1] In the end, it is as difficult to imagine Simone de Beauvoir's effort to find a totally new life style without the stifling and sterile atmosphere of her childhood as it is to envisage Simone Weil's writings on love and affection without the tenderness and depth of her bonds with her family.

Simone de Beauvoir and Simone Weil both spent their late teens in study with the greatest teacher of their generation, "Alain" (Emile-Auguste Chartier). Both were deeply influenced for life by this remarkable pedagogue. The key to Alain's teaching was in his determination to instill critical habits of mind in his students. He believed that students did not truly "acquire" ideas until they had digested them and re-expressed them in their own words. Thus his preference for assigning "topos," or take-home essay examinations, to his students which forced them to formulate their own (not "correct") answers to knotty questions. Simone Weil's brilliance in composing original and penetrating "topos" came from her unusual capacity for examining problems in a remarkably attentive way. Whether it was a mathematical problem or one of the complex moral issues Alain favoured (e.g., "Discuss the place of violence in Western History"), Simone Weil's remarkable ability simply to contemplate the subject until she surpassed generations of past analysts quickly made her one of Alain's favourites. And it is understandable how Simone could be so

---

1 She saw fatherhood as helping to reveal the nature of the universe: "The best support for faith is the guarantee that, if we ask our Father for bread, he does not give us a stone." "Reflections on the Right Use of School Studies," in *Waiting on God*, translated by Emma Craufurd (London, 1959), 68.

taken with a teacher whose interest in a wide range of subjects produced a host of unorthodox reflections. Such a process coincided well with her evolving interests and her entire personality.

Simone de Beauvoir's affinity for the teaching of Alain, in turn, proceeded from her determination to acquire total freedom from her cloying background. One need only point to the eloquent celebration of freedom which graces the opening lines of her memoirs on her first days of autonomy in Paris:

> The most intoxicating aspect of my return to Paris in September, 1929, was the freedom I now possessed. I had dreamed of it since childhood. . . . I have recorded elsewhere my passionate longing for it as a student. Now, suddenly, it was mine. . . . From the moment I opened my eyes every morning I was lost in a transport of delight.[2]

And the anarchical, vigorously independent style of Alain's teachings also fit in well with the orientation of her close friend, Jean-Paul Sartre:

> . . . I kept on good terms with my parents, but they no longer had any real hold over me. Sartre had never known his father, and neither his mother nor his grandmother had ever represented authority in his eyes. In a sense we both lacked a real family, and we had elevated this contingency into a principle. Here we were encouraged by Cartesian rationalism, which we had picked up from Alain. . . . There were no scruples, no feelings of respect or loyal affection that would stop us from making up our minds by the pure light of reason—and of our own desires . . . we believed ourselves to consist of pure reason and pure will.[3]

While Simone Weil remained a far more "dutiful" daughter than did Simone de Beauvoir, she too was attracted early to Alain's challenge to the most sacred beliefs of the French bourgeoisie, and his insistence on intellectual independence. Simone Weil too was soon engaged in an adolescent rebellion against middle class ways not unlike that of Simone de Beauvoir. In fact, on school days, Simone Weil's "revolt" was more visible and public than that of her daring feminist contemporary. Both young women quickly divorced themselves from the loathsome bourgeoisie by their clothing. Simone de Beauvoir's declaration of sartorial independence was, however, low key, if resolute:

2 Simone de Beauvoir, *The Prime of Life* (New York, 1973), 9.
3 Ibid., 15.

All my life I have been dressed in cotton or woolen frocks, so now I reacted by choosing silk-style materials instead—crepe de Chine and a ghastly fabric of embossed velvet called *velours frappé* which was all the rage that winter. Every morning I would make up with more dash than skill, smothering my face in powder, dabbing a patch of rouge on each cheek, and applying lipstick liberally. It struck me as ridiculous that anyone should dress up more elaborately on Sunday than during the week. Henceforth, I decided, every day was to be a holiday as far as I was concerned, and I always wore the same get-up, whatever the circumstance. It did occur to me that crepe de Chine and *velours frappé* were rather out of place in the corridors of a lycée, and that my evening shoes might have been less down at heel if I hadn't tramped the Paris pavements in them from morning till night; but I couldn't have cared less.[4]

Simone Weil, for her part, began dressing in an outlandish, even bizarre way that seemed to set her still further outside the crowd. Her school friend and biographer, Simone Pétrement, reconstructed her look in those days:

Her appearance, when she entered Khâgne (the preparatory course for the *Ecole Normale Supérieure*), was already nearly what it would be for the rest of her life. A small, thin face, which seemed devoured by her hair and glasses. The fine, delicate nose, the dark eyes with their bold look, the neck which strained forward, all gave the impression of a passionate, almost indiscreet curiosity; but her full mouth conveyed gentleness and kindness. . . . Her body was thin, her gestures lively but often clumsy. She wore clothes with a masculine cut, always the same outfit (a sort of suit with a very wide skirt and a long narrow jacket), and always flat-heeled shoes. She never wore a hat, which at that time was very unusual in the French bourgeoisie. All of this made for a singular personality in the image of the revolutionary intelligentsia and one which, for that or some other reason, had a way of irritating people, sometimes to the point of rage, and still does irritate them.[5]

Decades later, Simone Weil's attire—as her brother later observed—would have been a quite normal "beatnik" costume. But in those days even Simone Weil's friends were puzzled at her dress, at her apparent rejection of her frail beauty, and at her determination to appear as masculine as possible.[6] Even her admired mentor Alain, as Simone

4 Ibid., 11.
5 Pétrement, *Weil*, 1: 65.
6 Ibid., 67-88.

Pétrement recalled, would wonder about this extra-terrestrial crea-
ture sitting in the front row:

> It is possible that Alain himself at first felt a bit of peasant distrust in
> the presence of a creature so unearthly and so strange. Later I
> learned that he called her "The Martian." (I do not know if she ever
> knew this.) Later he explained that this name meant "that she had
> nothing in common with us and was sovereignly judging us all."[7]

Thus, in appearance, Simone Weil was the greater rebel, as she am-
bled through the Latin Quarter, her pockets stuffed with revolutionary literature, while Simone de Beauvoir appeared a bit too "chic"
and feminine. In fact, however, at a time when it took enormous
courage—even for someone not from a rigid provincial Catholic
family—Simone de Beauvoir had begun to live openly with Sartre,
while Simone Weil returned home alone from heaven-storming debates in Boul' Mich' cafés.

Simone de Beauvoir was impressed by Simone Weil's more public rebellion—and by her unusual reputation for empathy with the
poor and afflicted. She sought out the acquaintance of Simone Weil,
and was rejected in turn, as she recalled in her *Memoirs of a Dutiful
Daughter*:

> While preparing to enter *Normale* she was taking the same exami-
> nations at the Sorbonne as I. She intrigued me because of her great
> reputation for intelligence and her bizarre clothes; she would stroll
> around in the courtyard of the Sorbonne, escorted by a band of
> Alain's old students; she always had a copy of *Libre Propos* in one
> pocket of her jacket and a copy of *L'Humanité* in the other. A great
> famine had just begun to devastate China, and I was told that on
> hearing the news she had wept; these tears commanded my respect
> even more than her philosophical talents. I envied her for having a
> heart which could beat right across the world. One day I managed to
> approach her. I don't remember how the conversation began; she
> declared in no uncertain terms that one thing alone mattered in
> today's world: the Revolution that would feed all the people on
> earth. I retorted, no less peremptorily, that the problem was not to
> make men happy, but to find a meaning for their existence. She
> looked me up and down: "It's easy to see that you've never gone
> hungry," she said. Our relationship stopped there. I realized that
> she had catalogued me as a "middle-class spiritualist," and I was
> annoyed. . . . I believed myself emancipated from my social class.[8]

7 Alain, "Journal" (unpublished). Cited in Pétrement, *Weil*, 1: 65.
8 *Mémoires d'une jeune fille rangée* (Paris, 1958), 236-37.

Simone de Beauvoir was, by all accounts, a rather imperious and formidable young woman by this time, and not in the habit of being summarily dismissed by her peers. The two great contemporaries never did get to know one another and compare their two exigencies face to face. But Simone de Beauvoir did not forget "the Martian," and the rigour and force of her concern for her fellow men—and the contempt for Beauvoir's own more metaphysical concerns. Simone de Beauvoir's *Memoirs* attest to the rarity of strong social commitments among the young intellectuals of Paris—apart from a handful of Communists, such as Paul Nizan or Georges Politzer. And a persistent theme of Beauvoir's or Sartre's memories of the thirties was their oddly detached fascination with their fellow intellectuals who displayed this form of altruism in an authentic form. Simone Weil was spectacular in this regard.

The indirect liaison between the two Simones in subsequent years was a common friend (who would also become one of the best known women writers of their generation), Colette Audry. Audry, a pretty, dark-haired young Communist with quick lively eyes and close-cropped hair, also dressed "in an off-handedly masculine way, affecting a felt hat and a suede jacket." But, like Simone de Beauvoir, she was an aspiring novelist. Paul Nizan, the young Communist novelist who was a close friend of Sartre, warmly recommended her to Simone de Beauvoir and the two young women soon became close friends. Colette Audry, like Nizan, was trying to combine literary creation and Communist commitment and studied the works of Marx and Rosa Luxemburg as well as the art of the novel. But like some others of the keenest intellectuals of her generation, she belonged to a Trotskyist splinter group rather than to the French Communist Party, and there she had regular contact with Simone Weil.[9] Weil would, with her articles in the reviews *La Révolution prolétarienne* and *La Critique sociale* during the years 1932-33, establish herself as one of the most original and brilliant young non-Stalinist Marxist thinkers in France.[10]

Since Sartre and Simone de Beauvoir maintained a genuine, if relatively detached and uncommitted, interest in left-wing thought throughout the 1930s, it was normal that they should have heard of the political ideas of Simone Weil. But Simone Weil was determined to be more than a dispassionate intellectual, and already during 1931-32 she was working out the concrete implications of her social ideas—to

9   Beauvoir, *Prime*, 143-44.
10   See below, chapter 2.

the amazement of Colette Audry. Simone de Beauvoir recalled Audry
relating various stories about the peculiar actions of the "Martian":

> Colette Audry sometimes spoke of Simone Weil to me; and though I
> felt no great sympathy for her, this unknown woman's existence
> was forced upon my consciousness. She was a university teacher at
> Le Puy; it was said that she lived in a truck-drivers' hostel, and on
> the first of every month would put her entire salary packet out on
> the table and let anyone help themselves. In order to act as leader of
> a strike delegation and present their claims, she herself had worked
> alongside the railwaymen. Conduct such as this got her into trouble
> both with the local mayor and with her pupils' parents, and she had
> very nearly been run out of the university. Her intelligence, her
> asceticism, her total commitment, and her sheer courage—all these
> filled me with admiration; though I knew that, had she met me, she
> would have been very far from reciprocating my attitude. I could
> not absorb her into my universe, and this seemed to constitute a
> vague threat to me.[11]

Why should Simone Weil's "intelligence, asceticism, total commitment, and sheer courage" both "fill with admiration," and pose a
"vague threat to" Simone de Beauvoir? Certainly intelligence, asceticism, commitment, and courage were central values for herself and
Sartre, and those qualities account for the strong admiration which
Beauvoir could not help sharing with Audry for their unusual contemporary. The "vague threat" is less easy to understand and one
wonders if memoirs written twenty-five years later can be considered
completely reliable on this point. A theme running through them,
however, is the feeling of uneasiness which an intelligent individual
with strong political commitments caused in a couple who remained
pure intellectuals, seeking a "meaning" for human existence sooner
than addressing its sufferings and misfortunes.

In any case, the paths of Simone Weil and Simone de Beauvoir
would diverge more and more. After working in several factories in
the Paris region during 1934 and 1935 in an effort to understand the lot
of factory workers, Weil became concerned with the conflict in Spain
which broke out in July of 1936. In the beginning of August she took a
train for the Republican Front in Barcelona. There she sought difficult
and dangerous assignments to aid the anti-Franquist cause. Sartre and
Simone de Beauvoir were also staunchly pro-Republican, but their
reaction had necessarily been different from that of Weil (or Colette
Audry, who had also left to give speeches in Spain), as Beauvoir later

11 Beauvoir, *Prime*, 151.

recalled: "There was no question of our going to Spain ourselves; nothing in our previous background inclined us to such headstrong action." Moreover, as Simone de Beauvoir also later reflected, a concrete idealistic commitment like that of Simone Weil in the Spanish fighting could be ill-advised and foolhardy:

> . . . unless one got into some clearly defined technical or political job, there was a danger of being a nuisance rather than a help. Simone Weil had crossed the frontier determined to serve with the infantry; but when she asked for a gun they put her in the kitchens, where she spilled a bowl of boiling oil all over her feet.[12]

This is, in fact, a caricature of Simone Weil's reception at the front, and the circumstances of her grave injury there,[13] and there is the suggestion that Simone de Beauvoir's justification of her own "detachment" was a bit too strident, that the "foolhardiness" of Simone Weil remained a threat.

While Simone de Beauvoir most often described Simone Weil in her memoirs as a bizarre and incomprehensible personality, in her last reference to her in the 1930s she not only acknowledged an obsession with her (which she had not hinted at earlier), but also a remarkable esteem. The context was Sartre's chiding his friend for her "timidity" in her laborious, largely unsuccessful efforts as a novelist:

> "Look," he said, with sudden vehemence, "why don't you put *yourself* into your writing? You're more interesting than all those Renées and Lisas."
> "I'd never dare do that," I said. To put my raw, undigested self into a book, to lose perspective, compromise myself—no, I couldn't do it, I found the whole idea terrifying. "Screw up your courage," Sartre told me, and kept pressing the point.[14]

In her effort to isolate her true self, Simone de Beauvoir soon realized that she had become excessively dependent on Sartre: "Ever since Sartre and I had met, I had shoved off the responsibility for justifying my existence onto him." She then decided that the only solution for her would be to "accomplish some deed for which I alone, and no one else, must bear the consequences"—and not just any deed: in her typically radical and uncompromising style, she concluded

12   Ibid., 349.
13   In fact, Simone Weil was given a rifle at the front. Her grave burns resulted from her falling into a cooking pot of boiling oil buried to hide the fire glow from the enemy.
14   Beauvoir, *Prime*, 380.

that "nothing . . . short of an aggravated crime could bring me true independence."

The "metaphysical aspect of murder" came to fascinate her: "I saw myself in the dock, facing judge, prosecutor, jury, and a crowd of spectators, bearing the consequences of an act which I recognized as my handiwork, and bearing it alone." It was then that her thoughts turned to her fellow student who had humiliated her in the courtyard of the Sorbonne some years before:

> An alien personality revealed itself to me in all its irreducible actuality. Through jealousy and envy I committed some crime which put me at this person's mercy, and achieved my own safety by destroying the other. Because of the awed admiration she inspired in me at a distance, I had thought of using Simone Weil as a model for the protagonist I aimed to set up against me.[15]

Sartre rejected this notion of an ultimate protagonist for his friend. The former seemed less troubled by the legitimacy of the novelist's vocation over against the activist's, and he told Beauvoir that it was illegitimate to consider a woman "devoted to the art of communication" as "an exclusively inward turning personality" when juxtaposed to the empathic, socially concerned Weil. She agreed, and dropped the idea.

After the war and occupation Sartre came to have more and more sympathy for (what Simone de Beauvoir remembered to be) his friend's doubts over the legitimacy of disinterested intellectual and artistic endeavor. The two came to have an increasing admiration for friends, such as Paul Nizan and Colette Audry, who had combined artistic and intellectual researches with political commitment. The "vague threat" and "awed admiration" which Simone Weil had inspired in Simone de Beauvoir were put to rest in her memoirs when she said, in retrospect, that she and Sartre had probably always had a bad conscience about their apoliticism in the thirties but were unable to be open about it. This may partly explain the paradoxical fear and admiration which an activist intellectual antipode like Simone Weil could evoke.

A juxtaposition of the careers of the two Simones, then, indicates that while the two sharply differed after their student days, they drew closer with the war as Beauvoir began to combine her artistic and intellectual endeavours more and more with concrete social concerns. This, however, does not suffice to assess the fate of two very

15 Ibid., 382.

different women. Simone de Beauvoir's basic search was always for independence, liberty, and meaning for her existence and those of others—in a word: for self-fulfillment. Simone Weil was, from her childhood, one of those very rare human beings who was both extremely intellectualist and selfless. Simone de Beauvoir's search for meaning led her to conclude that existence could be found meaningful only in a commitment to others: to Sartre, the proletariat, the cause of women. Simone Weil's commitment to others preceded everything, and the less she became concerned for herself and her own sense of "meaning," the more she acquiesced in what she called her condition of slave. This later acquiescence was, and would remain, totally different from the position of Simone de Beauvoir. In fact, it was the "slavishness" of so much of her Catholic background which partly inspired Beauvoir's later engagements in liberation movements.

Simone de Beauvoir may have ended up, in retrospect, where Simone Weil began. But, paradoxical as it may seem, it can also be said that Simone Weil ended up where Simone de Beauvoir began—in what a friend of Sartre's called "that bestial slave religion," Catholicism. The schoolyard snubbing was both prelude and summary.

2
THE INSUFFICIENCY OF POLITICS

A Brilliant Theoretical Insight

Albert Camus wrote of Simone Weil's essay "Reflections on the Causes of Liberty and of Social Oppression" that "Western political and social thought has not produced anything more penetrating and prophetic."[1] But, however penetrating and prophetic, was Simone Weil an important *political* thinker? A scholarly study of her "ideology and politics" concluded that the most coherent period of her life, politically speaking, was brief: from the end of 1928, date of her entry into the *Ecole Normale*, and her beginning factory work in December 1934 and her period of political militancy was only from 1931-34.[2] Thus, in an important way Simone Weil had "outgrown" politics at twenty-five—at an early point in her remarkable intellectual production. After that her thought—like that of Camus himself—was too broad in range to be classified simply as political. She did write some important and original essays in politics, but we shall approach these from the perspective of the working out of her general system of thought rather than as mature, definitive analysis. Once she conceived of the first premises of her thought system it seems clear that she no longer considered traditional essays

---

1 "Note à l'éditeur," in Simone Weil, *Oppression et liberté* (Paris, 1955), 8.
2 Cf. Philippe Dujardin, *Simone Weil: Idéologie et politique* (Grenoble, 1975), 103.

17

on politics broad enough in scope and focus, and it is this realization
of hers, and how she came to it, which interests us here.

Simone Weil's generation came to maturity in the Great Depression, in a period of extremist politics of the Left and Right, and a
growing threat of war. The early 1930s brought economic crisis and
massive unemployment to France, and a growing frustration with the
inability of the Third Republic to deal effectively with the internal
and external crises. On February 6, 1934, the right-wing groups—and
some Communists—engaged in a massive riot in the streets of Paris
which brought out a vast manifestation of the Left in reply. The year
1935 brought the Italian invasion of Ethiopia and the end of many
illusions regarding the nature of Italian Fascism. In 1936 there was the
victory of the anti-fascist Popular Front coalition government in
France and, a few weeks later, Franco helped precipitate the rebellion
against the Spanish Republic. In sum, the very years in which Simone
Weil gradually withdrew from political militancy were years of growing political polarization and militancy among her peers. These were,
in the words of one historian, "years of desperation" for the French
and their social and political thought reflected this.[3]

Simone Weil was instinctively attracted to left-wing political
causes from a very young age and soon travelled in or joined various
Marxist circles. Increasingly, however, she became concerned with
the relationship of technology to modern society and particularly to
the working class. Her own experience in factory and agricultural
work, coupled with her realization of the left-wing leaders' ignorance
about the realities of these situations, fostered disillusionment with
Marxism and, later, revolutionary syndicalism too. Her experiences
in the Spanish Civil War and her observations on the reasons for
the progress of fascism led her to more and more reflection outside
of traditional political categories: about the technocracies which
characterized all modern societies—communist, fascist or capitalist; about the lack of meaning in factory work; about means for
creating a proletarian condition more bearable and free. While there
were several thinkers of her generation who were moved by similar
concerns to abandon religious or philosophical concerns for the directly political, Weil went in the opposite direction. Almost alone in
her intellectual generation she proceeded from Marxism, via anarchism, towards religious and metaphysical analyses. That she proceeded in this direction with great lucidity and logic is what we hope
to demonstrate in this chapter.

3 Cf. H. Stuart Hughes, *The Obstructed Path: French Social Thought in the Years of
Desperation, 1930-1960* (New York, 1969).

Simone Weil was, she told a friend, a Bolshevik from the age of ten.[4] Her school friends remembered her having avant-garde political ideas and a commitment to the extreme Left from her late teens. The root of her first political engagements seems to have been her empathy for the suffering and oppressed: she had that "heart capable of beating across the Continents" for her fellow human beings which so impressed Simone de Beauvoir. At first glance this might seem perfectly normal and appropriate as an inspiration for a Marxist commitment but when one places her in the context of her generation and milieu it was somewhat unusual. *Normaliens* of comfortable middle-class backgrounds have become Marxists for a host of reasons, but compassion for the disfavoured was not particularly high on the list at this time. The novels of Sartre and Simone de Beauvoir, with their colourful and lucid depictions of the Parisian intellectual milieu, are quite revealing in their portraits of the "Marxists." Some came to Marxism through intellectual snobbery, others to fulfill a need (on the Right as well as the Left) for commitment. For many it seemed the best way of heading off the threat of fascism or war; for others it was the total, coherent explanation of history and society they craved. But, above all, it was hatred of French middle-class society, a need to break up bourgeois culture, that was an important factor in the Marxism of the leaders of "the generation of 1930" in France.[5] Many of Simone Weil's friends were—like Simone de Beauvoir—in rebellion against the society in which they were raised. This contempt and hatred for the bourgeoisie drove some *normaliens* toward fascism, others toward the French Communist Party. But the roots of the commitments were similar and compassion or pity had little to do with them. It did not take Simone Weil long to recognize that her own deepest concerns were very different from those of many of her compatriots, and this had an important effect on her subsequent evolution. The compassion she felt for the working class had its origins in that capacity for empathic attention to others which characterized her entire life. And that faculty, when applied to the condition of the proletariat, quickly made a maverick Marxist of Simone Weil.

One of the things which impressed Simone de Beauvoir about Simone Weil, as we have seen, was her effort—already in the days of

---

4 Testimony of Doctor Bercher, a comrade during her years at the review *La Révolution prolétarienne*, cited in Dujardin, *Weil*, 75.

5 Cf. David Caute, *Communism and the French Intellectuals, 1914-1960* (London, 1964); Jean-Louis Loubet del Bayle, *Les Non-conformistes des années 30* (Paris, 1969); and John Hellman, *Emmanuel Mounier and the New Catholic Left, 1930-1950* (Toronto, 1981).

her beginnings as a teacher—not only to support workers' causes but also to try to establish direct contact with the workers themselves. Yet Simone Weil was frail and awkward, an intellectual to the fingertips, and the product of a home which protected her from the harshness and vulgarity of factory workers' life. It was no easy matter for her to befriend auto workers, miners, beet farmers, and Breton fishermen. With a great effort of will, she was able to do just this—and, as many of her admirers found when they retraced her steps, she had gained the affection and respect of these proletarians as well.

What set off Simone Weil very quickly from her comrades was her youthful determination not only to talk about the working class in the courtyard of the Sorbonne but to get to know the day-to-day situation of workers. This did not mean reading about them in the British Museum, or learning about them vicariously through an acute observer, like the young Engels, who knew the proletarian life. Almost unique in her generation of intellectuals (and our own), she decided to get to know the workers' life firsthand, by sharing it with them, despite the fact that few in her milieu seemed more ill-suited, physically or by family background, for such an initiative.

In March 1932, as a beginning philosophy teacher, keen and green, near the industrial centre of St. Etienne, she insisted on visiting a local mine and working with an air hammer. This, and similar experiences, inspired her to a set of reflections which quickly made a reputation for originality for this twenty-four-year-old. She wrote not long thereafter:

> It will not suffice for the miner to expropriate the companies to become master of the mine. The political revolution, the economic revolution, will not become real unless they are succeeded by a technical revolution which will reestablish, in the very interior of the mine and the factory, the control which the worker must exercise over his work conditions.[6]

The focus of Simone's analysis would remain in all of her political writings: the individual worker in his total living context. A great deal was being written, in her circle, about the plight of the working class, but very few of her fellow intellectuals had thought of doing what seemed so self-evidently necessary, simple, and essential to her: to go into the work place and see what the workers' lot was like. Holding an air hammer all day was rough work, whatever the financial remuneration or ideology of the state. What was vital and necessary for miners,

6 Cited in Pétrement, *Weil*, 1: 258-59.

she thought, was the possibility to make air-hammering as bearable as possible. This seems obvious enough, but why had not the revolutionary leadership or intelligentsia said it? Why had none of them even thought seriously about holding an air hammer, or worried about ameliorating the conditions of men doing this work?

In August 1933 Weil carried these reflections further in a widely read article in the avant-garde, anti-Stalinist Communist review *Révolution prolétarienne*. The problems faced by someone manning an air hammer tended to be largely the same whatever the regime—despite the enormous tensions in Europe between "capitalism" and "Communism." She sought to show that the principle axiom of the revolutionaries whereby there were only two forms for the state—the capitalist state and the worker state—was false. The modern state was neither "capitalist" nor "worker" controlled, but in fact was of a third sort. Fascism was no more the "last card of capitalism" than Stalinism was (as her Trotskyist friends argued) a bureaucratic deformation of the proletarian dictatorship. Both were in fact new social forms which represented the true revolution of the twentieth century: a revolution of *cadres*, of bureaucratic elites, not of the proletariat.

In order to illustrate this she presented a harsh but telling portrait of the Soviet Union:

> Throughout history men have struggled, suffered and died to free the oppressed. Their efforts, when they did not remain sterile, have never led to anything except the replacing of one oppressive regime by another....
>
> [In the Soviet Union]... there is a professional bureaucracy, freed from responsibility, recruited by co-option, and possessing, through the concentration in its hands of all economic and political power, a strength hitherto unknown in the annals of history.
>
> ... to call a State a "workers' State" when you go on to explain that each worker in it is put economically and politically at the complete disposal of a bureaucratic caste, sounds like a bad joke.
>
> ... Certainly, Marx never foresaw anything of this kind. But not even Marx is more precious to us than the truth.[7]

Once again, as in so many other areas, Weil's analysis was far ahead of her time. Her contemporaries saw the basic difficulties in Soviet Communism as due to the Russian heritage, the capricious dictatorship of Stalin, the brutal suppression of the kulaks, the stifling of

---

7 "Prospects," *La Révolution prolétarienne*, No. 150 (August 25, 1933). Reprinted in Simone Weil, *Oppression and Liberty*, translated by Arthur Wills and John Petrie (London, 1972), 2, 4, 6.

opposition, the denial of civil liberties, etc. Weil, in a Europe more and more polarized by ideologies, took the original position that the oppression of miners in the mid-twentieth century was far more complex, and far less understood, than the great leaders of the Left pretended. She argued that the proletariat had enormous difficulties in regimes on all areas of the political spectrum in their struggle to gain direction of their work and lives, and thus the traditional notion of class struggle as the key to understanding the proletarian situation was no longer adequate. For the working class the technocrat elites—whether in Communist, fascist, or capitalist regimes—were becoming the great oppressor. This was so because these men—in Russia, Germany, and the United States—were gaining unprecedented control over others. In her view, however well-intentioned the *cadres* might be, it remained true that "all exclusive, uncontrolled power becomes oppressive in the hands of those who have the monopoly of it."[8] Marx, as she said, had not foreseen this "new species of oppression, an oppression exercised in the name of management."[9]

Simone Weil's analysis of the roots of technocratic oppression, and denunciation of what Michel Crozier, decades later, would call *The Bureaucratic Phenomenon*,[10] did not settle for a facile blaming of specific parties or personalities, or even the technocrats themselves. Rather she suggested some origins of the problem in the process of technological evolution itself, in the dynamics of what Jacques Ellul, years afterward, would describe as *The Technological Society*.[11] She was able to link the workers, technicians, engineers, and scientists in a common plight which most Marxists had not even considered:

> ... workers are becoming more and more lacking in technical knowledge, the technicians'... proficiency is in many cases limited to a quite restricted field;... they have even set about producing specialized engineers—just like ordinary unskilled men—in a certain category of machines.... Moreover... the technicians are ignorant of the theoretical basis of the knowledge which they employ. The scientists, in their turn, not only remain out of touch with technical problems, but... deprived of that general view of things which is the very essence of theoretical culture. One could count on one's fingers the number of scientists throughout the world with a general idea of the history and development of their particular

8   Weil, "Prospects," *Oppression*, 15.
9   Ibid., 9.
10 Michel Crozier, *The Bureaucratic Phenomenon* (Chicago, 1964).
11 Jacques Ellul, *The Technological Society* (New York, 1964).

science: there is none who is really competent as regards sciences other than his own. As science forms an indivisible whole, one may say that there are no longer, strictly speaking, scientists but only unskilled hands doing scientific work, cogs in a whole which their minds are quite incapable of embracing.[12]

Thus Simone Weil was able to suggest possible lines of analysis for the failures of the Soviet Union from the workers' point of view. And, here, her suggestions foreshadowed the efforts of men like Ellul and Marcuse decades later: the oppression of modern workers was not a phenomenon for which capitalism was primarily responsible—or fascism, or an "aberrant" Stalinism. Rather a new social form was emerging in the twentieth century which seemed invariably elitist and authoritarian in relation to the workers, no matter what the ideology of the State power. The focus for the liberation of workers, she suggested, should be the actual working conditions of those one was presuming to liberate. And here, in the end, her position was less critical of the bureaucrats themselves than hopeful that new paths of study, new foci of reflection, could be brought forward to relieve the oppression which seemed so rooted in modern life. A turn toward some total perspective on the place of science in modern life and the direction scientific research and development were taking was just one of her unique directions. Marx had not foreseen this as a problem, but the truth of oppression was there nevertheless, and even if this raised some questions about the adequacy of Marxism, "not even Marx" should prevent the Marxist social analyst from a facing up to the facts.

The ideas in this essay quickly established the twenty-four-year-old school teacher's reputation as a brilliant and innovative political theorist. Non-Stalinist Marxist intellectuals were lavish in their praise: Marcel Martinet called it a work of genius and said nothing comparable had been written since Rosa Luxemburg; Boris Souvarine called her the only real thinker the workers' movement had had for many years.[13] A strong dissenting voice, however, was that of Léon Trotsky, who denounced her ideas in an article the following October.[14] (Later the frail normalien philosophy teacher—to the astonishment of her friends—had it out with the founder of the Red Army in her parents' apartment, which she had placed at his disposition.

12 Weil, "Prospects,"Oppression, 13.
13 Pétrement, Weil, 1: 352.
14 Léon Trotsky, "La quatrième internationale et l'U.R.S.S. (la nature de classe de l'Etat soviétique)," La Vérité, No. 175 (October 13, 1933).

Trotsky ended up saying: "I see you disagree with me in almost everything. Why do you put me up in your house? Do you belong to the Salvation Army?").[15]

To understand the ability of this young, relatively sheltered and inexperienced intellectual to produce a political essay of such originality and power, we may return to her faculty of empathic concern. Who, aside from Simone Weil, among "spokesmen of the working class" in her generation, was actually paying attention to individual miners in St. Etienne? Yet concentration on the reality of air hammers and reflection on the context in which mining was done led to new ideas about the relation between man and machinery, technology, and the general direction which the "new" society in the twentieth century was taking.

In November 1933, Weil suggested that the very criticism which the young Marx had applied to the religious culture of mid-nineteenth-century Europe should now be turned upon the scientific culture which characterized the West a century later. "Science" she wrote "had become the most modern form of consciousness of mankind which has not yet found self or has once again lost self—to apply Marx's telling dictum concerning religion." Science was becoming the theology of the bureaucracy-ridden society which she had denounced; science had taken the position which religion had once occupied for Marx.[16] Therefore, she thought, Marx's excellent observation that the "criticism of religion is the premise of all criticism" had to be recast for the new situation, and extended to include modern science: "socialism will not even be conceivable as long as science has not been stripped of its mystery."[17]

Like her master Alain, Simone Weil had great admiration for Descartes, and particularly for Descartes' effort to found a science without mystery. She too admired such great unity and simplicity of method, in which everyone would be able to understand how results had been obtained, so that every schoolboy would have the feeling of inventing science anew. Descartes had advocated a School of Arts and Crafts, where each artisan would learn fully to understand the theoretical basis of his own craft. With this initiative, Weil charged, Descartes

15 Recollections of André Weil in appendix to Simone Weil, *Gateway to God*, edited by David Raper (London, 1974), 154.

16 Weil alludes here to Marx's early work—the so-called "humanist" period—when he was under the influence of the critical theology of Bruno Bauer and Ludwig Feuerbach. Representative tracts by Marx include *Die Heilige Familie* and *Die Deutsche Ideologie*.

17 "Lenin's 'Materialism and Empiriocriticism,'" *Critique Sociale* (November 1933), in Weil, *Oppression*, 35.

"showed himself to be more socialist, in the matter of culture, than all Marx's disciples have been."[18]

Thus Simone Weil was able to link her violent critique of the oppressive and anti-worker tendencies of the Soviet Union, her call for a critical analysis of the roots and direction of the new technological, bureaucratic social form which was arising beyond ideologies, with her insistence that, in the twentieth century, science had become the new religion. And the spokesmen of the working class, the intellectuals of the Left, who should have recognized this new form of oppression and attacked its bases, only reinforced it. In her words, ". . . the theorists of the socialist movement . . . never think at all of undermining the privileges of the intellectual caste—far from it; instead, they elaborate a complicated and mysterious doctrine which serves to maintain the bureaucratic oppression at the heart of the working class movement."[19] Here it is important to note, in view of her subsequent evolution, that Weil has already agreed with Marx that the criticism of religion was "the premise of all criticism" as far as Western culture was concerned. Marx, however, had thought that, in his day, thanks to Feuerbach, the Young Hegelians, et al., the "criticism of religion was in the main complete." Weil thought that, almost one hundred years later, the "criticism of religion" necessary for human liberty was only beginning, due to circumstances which Marx had not foreseen: the elaboration of a "new theology" of science and its employment by elites, of the Left and Right, of the East and West, to reinforce their own authority, privileges, and power. Therefore, she argued, the criticism of religion begun by Marx had to be extended to embrace the new social forms, the new technology.

What Marx Had Not Foreseen

The opening of Simone Weil's most important political essay, "Reflections Concerning the Causes of Liberty and Social Oppression (1934) seems to mimic the apocalyptic "spectre of Communism stalking Europe" with which Marx and Engels began their *Communist Manifesto* (1848). While Marx and Engels described incipient class war and impending social revolution, Simone Weil described a situation in which the succeeding century had brought new forces into play. There were new demons which the great fathers of communism had not envisaged in their neat Manichean view of the world divided between good and evil, workers and exploiters, communists and capitalists:

18 Ibid., 35-36.
19 Ibid., 36.

The present period is one of those when everything that seems normally to constitute a reason for living dwindles away, when one must . . . call everything into question again. That the triumph of authoritarian and nationalist movements should blast almost everywhere the hopes that well-meaning people had placed in democracy and pacifism is only a part of the evil from which we are suffering; it is far deeper and widespread . . . . Work is no longer done with the proud consciousness that one is being useful, but with the humiliating and agonizing feeling of enjoying a privilege bestowed by a temporary stroke of fortune . . . that one enjoys, in short, a job . . . . Technical progress seems to have gone bankrupt, since instead of happiness it has only brought the masses that physical and moral wretchedness in which we see them floundering. . . . As for scientific progress, it is difficult to see what can be the use of piling up still more knowledge onto a heap already much too vast to be able to be embraced even in the minds of specialists; . . . our forefathers were mistaken in believing in the spread of enlightenment, since all that can be revealed to the masses is a miserable caricature of modern scientific culture . . . . Waiting for that which is to come is no longer a matter of hope, but of anguish.[20]

This paragraph, for all its timeless gravity, neatly pinpoints several phenomena of the 1930s which, indeed, the *Communist Manifesto* had not foreseen. She beholds the emergence of fascism and Hitlerism with their new styles of "revolution," the meaninglessness of so much modern work, the dislocations masked by the benefits of modern technical progress, and the fragmentation of modern scientific research and the consequent lack of comprehension of its procedures and purposes on the part of the population at large. Since it was more important to remain conscious of the workers' condition than to echo Marx, all of these problems had to be squarely faced—even by devotees of Marx—or there would be no social revolution.

We have already noted some deviant views toward revolutionary thought articulated by Weil in her first precocious essays: the notion that the old revolutionary vision dividing the world into capitalist and communist states did not suffice to explain the new social form which the modern state represented, that the Soviet Union was an example of a bureaucratic technocratic state along these lines, and that there could be no Socialism unless elitist technology and over-specialist science were frankly confronted. Several of the innovative lines of analysis of her first essay were simply carried further in "Reflections," with an eye toward elaborating the inadequacies of

20 Weil, "Reflections Concerning the Causes of Liberty and Social Oppression," in Weil, *Oppression*, 37-38.

Marxism in the new situation and the guidelines for the renewal of revolutionary thought and action.

One of Weil's first contentions in this essay was that Bolshevik leaders had quickly realized that they were powerless to bring about the workers' democracy which Marx had foreshadowed. Making the best of things, they quickly justified their "supreme disdain for democratic ideas" by arguing that all progress in productive forces caused humanity to advance along the road leading to emancipation, even if it was at the cost of temporary oppression.[21] Weil contested this blind faith in the evolution of productive forces. Could one, she asked, continue to defend the equally sanguine assumption that tinkering with private property would, in itself, transform work in the mines and factories for those who are subjected to it? This, she argued, was a fundamental question regarding one's understanding of the forces which governed the historical evolution of our culture. It was not being confronted at all, either by revolutionaries or the intellectual leaders of the capitalist societies:

> ... if the present state of technique is insufficient to liberate the workers, is there, at any rate, a reasonable hope that unlimited development looms ahead, which would imply an unlimited increase in productivity? This is what everybody assumes, both among capitalists and socialists, without the smallest preliminary study of the question. It suffices that the productivity of human effort has increased in an unheard-of manner for the last three centuries. It is to be expected that this increase will continue at the same rate.[22]

Behind this assumption of unlimited increase in productivity, she thought, was the distortion of modern scientific culture which she had described earlier. Even Marx, whose dialectical method should have protected him from error on this point, misperceived it as well.

Behind this notion of unlimited increase in productivity lurked an even more basic assumption begging for critical examination: technical progress. Just what is technical progress? What factors play a part in it? How could these factors be examined independently? The first issue she raised in this regard (decades before the world energy crisis) was the utilization of natural sources of energy. Here was a garden in which the faithful romped in blissful ignorance, for:

21 Ibid., 43.
22 Ibid., 47.

... we do not know what new sources of energy we shall one day be able to use; but this does not mean to say that there can be prospects of unlimited progress in this direction... since the extraction of coal and petroleum becomes continually and automatically less profitable and more costly. What is more, the deposits at present known are destined to become exhausted at the end of a relatively short time. Perhaps new deposits will be found; ... in any case, their number will not be unlimited. We may also... discover new sources of energy; but there is nothing to guarantee that their utilization will call for less labour than the utilization of coal or heavy oils; the opposite is just as possible.... In this field it is chance which decides; for the discovery of a new and easily accessible source of energy... is not one of those things one is sure of reaching on a basis of thinking methodically and spending the necessary time thereon.[23]

Modern scientific culture had become the new religion, and part of this belief system was the blind idea that scientists could resolve the difficulties posed by the exhaustion of a set of natural sources of energy by coming up with the quick fix. Soberly she rejoined that the scientist seeking new sources of energy was "no more certain of coming across something economically advantageous in the course of his researches than is the explorer of arriving at fertile territory."[24] In the matter of energy, as in so many other areas of technical progress, the sort of critique which the young Marx and the Hegelian Left launched so effectively against religion was needed. Without such a critique, the prospect of workers' liberation would be even dimmer.

Weil began an analysis of the factors commonly associated with technical progress, trying to focus on each one separately: the "co-ordination of effort in time," "mechanization," "automation" were considered from various aspects. She could not justify the current faith that technical progress would eventually free men from labour—a belief which, she thought, characterized her age. On the contrary, she concluded that much modern optimism was misplaced. No technique, she argued, would ever relieve men of gaining their bread by the sweat of their brow. The metals from which the machines were made, in turn, required miners to mine them. Nor were the metals needed for the machines inexhaustible: "... men reproduce themselves, iron does not."[25]

23 Ibid., 47-48.
24 Ibid., 48.
25 Ibid., 50-52.

The complexity of the factors involved in technical progress, Simone Weil argued, necessarily raised questions about the utopian vision of the final stage of social evolution which Marx maintained. The superficiality of Marx's notion, in her view, was revealed by his facile faith in unlimited future productivity. Such an assumption required proof and seemed shaky under analysis. It was just another manifestation of the modern "religion" of science, and it had unfortunate, even pernicious, effects on the hopes of revolutionaries:

> . . . the possibility of future progress as far as concerns productivity is not beyond question: . . . to all appearances, we have at present as many reasons to expect diminishment as increase . . . . It is solely the frenzy produced by the speed of technical progress that has brought about the mad idea that work might one day become unnecessary. In the realm of pure science, this idea has found expression in the search for a "perpetual motion machine"—that is to say, a machine which would go on producing work indefinitely without ever consuming any . . . . The "higher stage of communism" regarded by Marx as the final term of social evolution, is, in effect, a utopia absolutely analogous with that of perpetual motion.
>
> It is in the name of this utopia that revolutionaries have shed their blood.[26]

In Weil's view the utopianism of Marxist revolutionaries had to be demythologized, just as the "opium" of religious aspirations had been denounced by Marx and his friends in the first half of the nineteenth century. A more tough-minded approach to revolutionary goals and aspirations was required in the mid-twentieth century.

What were genuine revolutionary aspirations in the twentieth century? Once again Weil saw clues in the point of view of the individual worker, not in vast ideological constructs: "What we should ask of the revolution is the abolition of social oppression."[27] She thought that Marx had demonstrated quite convincingly how big industry reduced workers to the position of a wheel in the factory, a mere instrument in the hands of his employers. But it was useless to believe, as did many Marxists, that technical progress would alleviate this problem. Rather, in her view, ". . . it is a question of knowing whether it is possible to conceive of an organization of production which, though powerless to remove the necessities imposed by nature . . . would enable these at any rate to be exercised without grinding down souls and bodies under oppression."[28] She agreed

26 Ibid., 54.
27 Ibid., 55.
28 Ibid., 56.

with Marx that the causes of oppression resided in the objective, material conditions. She simply wished to raise what was, in contemporary Marxist circles, a novel question—how oppression was tied in with production: "The problem is, in short, to know what it is that links oppression in general and each form of oppression in particular to the system of production; in other words, to succeed in grasping the mechanism of oppression, in understanding by what means it arises, subsists, transforms itself, by what means, perhaps, it might theoretically disappear."[29]

A failure to come to grips with the problem of oppression in modern production was, Simone Weil thought, fundamental to Marx and later Marxists. Marx failed to deal with these questions, and later Marxists had not even formulated them.[30] This was a grave omission, for when one studied history one noted that "among all the forms of social organization which history has to show, there are very few which appear to be really free from oppression; and these few are not very well known."[31] Because we live in such a "religious" age—with our mythologized scientific culture—revolutionaries had utopian faiths that prevented them from confronting the real problems of the working class.

There was another aspect to the inadequacy of Marxist analysis in this area. While Weil accepted Marx's insight that social existence was determined by the relations between man and nature established by production, "the only sound basis for any historical investigation"—she thought Marx had oversimplified the struggle between social classes by centring on the issue of mere material subsistence. In fact, social relationships were deeply perverted by oppression of all sorts: "Once society is divided up into men who command and men who execute, the whole of social life is governed by the struggle for power, and the struggle for subsistence only enters in as one factor, indispensable to be sure, of the former."[32] The insufficiency of Marx, then, was that he too narrowly centred his analysis of tensions in society on the struggle for the means of subsistence when this was simply one of the components of the real problem—the problem of power. Thus we can see how, for Simone Weil, the oppressive society in the Soviet Union might well have provided subsistence for all of its members, yet still fostered the most terrible abuse of

29 Ibid., 56-57.
30 Ibid., 58.
31 Ibid., 61.
32 Ibid., 71.

workers along with it. This, in Weil's eyes, would be the result of uncritical fidelity to the thought of Marx.

Weil made a serious effort to sketch a "theoretical picture" of a free society—beyond the Soviet Union, beyond Marx, and beyond the modern scientific culture and the technological society oppressing men in both East and West. It was not elaborated with any great precision or detail, but it was charged, nevertheless, with a quality that was central to all of the early political essays of the young school teacher: it was worker-centred. In contrast to the ethereal quality of so much political and social theory then and now, this section of the essay described the proletariat with an imagery and fervour which indicated that she knew whom she was talking about. This thinker had, if only for a time, shared their lot. To illustrate Marx's vagueness on relationships of production, she could contrast the work of fishermen, such as those she sailed with off the Breton coast, with that of the automobile assembly line men she knew in the Paris suburb. The "means of subsistence" of these men were not always the key issue for them—nor even their benefits, possibilities for recreation, or sense of permanence at the job:

> It is clear enough that one kind of work differs substantially from another by reason of something which has nothing to do with welfare, or leisure or security, and yet which claims each man's devotion; a fisherman battling against wind and waves in his little boat, although he suffers from cold, fatigue, lack of leisure and even sleep, danger and a primitive level of existence, has a more enviable lot than the manual worker on a production-line, who is nevertheless better off as regards nearly all these matters.[33]

And it was not only types of work, like that of the fisherman and the assembly-line worker, that she contrasted but also *how* men worked. Some ways of working subjected men to oppression, she thought, others allowed them significant liberty and a sense of community:

> ... a team of workers on a production line under the eye of a foreman is a sorry spectacle, whereas it is a fine sight to see a handful of workmen in the building trade, checked by some difficulty, ponder the problem each for himself, make various suggestions for dealing with it, and then apply the method conceived by one of them, who may or may not have any official authority over the remainder. At such moments the image of a free community appears almost in its purity.[34]

33 Ibid., 100-101.
34 Weil, "Reflections," in Weil, *Oppression*, 101.

In these two illustrations we see both the strength and weaknesses of the *agrégée* disciple of Alain turned student of factory workers. Simone Weil, steeped in classical literature, high-minded, remarkably courageous and independent, would, of course, find the lonely and stoical life of the lone fisherman essentially more attractive than a dull eight-hour factory shift. But would everyone? What was wrong with those sons of Breton fishermen who fled the high seas for the safe, regular, and relatively undemanding assembly line? And her description of the building workers recalls the study cells in the *Ecole Normale Supérieure*. Was every worker as eager to attack construction problems as the brilliant Simone Weil? For every auto worker keen to solve technical problems were there not a drove happy to escape that responsibility and let the foreman tell them what to do? Alain had insisted in the "Topo" system on the sacred character of independent thought and analysis. Would Alain have applied this to the nightshift at Renault? After working on one assembly line, Weil, as we shall see, admitted that she found what seemed a necessary relationship between goodness and intelligence in her fellow workers.[35]

But despite the intellectualism of this early essay one must concede Weil's prescience in arguing the case that technological society had made several of Marx's key analyses out-dated and simplistic. So many of her views, startling to Marxists in her day, are commonplace in our own. Who today would speak of "progress," for example, with the same assuredness that was common in her day? Or of unlimited productive capacities? Or the improving quality of workers' lives? Or the liberating features of modern technological society?

Simone Weil's prediction of the future of the technological society included the dark suggestion that even such terms as oppressor, oppressed, and social classes were losing their meaning in the face of the heartless "social machine" which was emerging.[36] Thus the old, generous, but rather simplistic view of the world held by revolutionaries had to be replaced with a fresh, clearer vision. As part of achieving this she suggested (again, decades before this was fashionable) an effort to demythologize science by, whenever possible, conceiving of and presenting scientific results "as merely a phase in the methodical activity of the mind," and for this purpose she suggested serious study of the history of science. The dissection of the

---

35 In her *Journal d'usine* she noted of her fellow workers: "... I have always found in these uneducated people generosity of heart and aptitude for general ideas in a direct functional relationship with one another" (La condition ouvrière [Paris, 1951], 145).

36 Weil, "Reflections," in Weil, *Oppression*, 108.

technological society, too, had to be approached in a new, determined way: "As for the technique, it ought to be studied in a thoroughgoing manner—its history, present state, and possibilities of development—and that from an entirely new point of view, which would no longer be that of output, but that of the relation between the worker and his work."[37] All of the reflections of Simone Weil on the situation of modern workers can be related to the new way in which she observed men working with air hammers in the mines of St. Etienne. In her generation of Marxists she was perhaps the first to truly look at these men, empathize with them, and do something direct about what she considered to be their genuine, day to day difficulties. This focus on working men provided the freshness and originality in her analysis, and in the entire set of views which proceed from it.

Factory Work
Politics became a "sinister joke" for Simone Weil when she thought back on all the great Bolshevik leaders—Lenin, Trotsky, *et al.*—who pretended to liberate the working class but who had never so much as set foot in a factory.[38] The basic problem which she began to study more and more was how to reconcile the organization which an industrial society required with suitable work and living conditions for a free proletariat. Despite the assurances on certain key issues which characterized her political essays, she decided she would have to have more first-hand knowledge of these conditions in order to be able to write about them with authority. Although she recognized that this experience would be particularly difficult for her (and, as her *Journal d'usine* indicates, it was),[39] she worked at various difficult and menial factory jobs in the Paris region during 1934 and 1935. Her experiences there—the empathy, courage and sensitivity she displayed—greatly added to the legend that now surrounds her personal life.

The extended factory experience confirmed, rather than altered, most of Weil's earlier political and social opinions. Her *Journal* observations indicate that her conviction as to the narrowness of scope of much political and social thought was reinforced, as was her scepticism about the efficacy of extant forms of political action. She noted with new clarity that despite the romantic sentiments and rhetoric of

37 Ibid., 110.
38 Pétrement, *Weil*, 2: 30.
39 Cf. Weil, *La Condition*, 45-145.

her revolutionary friends there was very little sense of fraternity among workers. (For example, the few kind personalities who offered to help or encourage her in some of her difficulties with machines new to her were indelibly etched on her memory.)[40] She grew disillusioned working with a group studying the "Plan" of the French Labour Union, the C.G.T., and discovering that even in the union movement—in which she had briefly placed her hopes after her disappointment with Marxist political parties—the entire mentality of the leadership was geared toward manipulating the workers according to its whims, via a strong central power.[41] With such a centralizing and elitist leadership, little hope could be placed in the true liberation of workers through the projects of the unions. She confessed that when one knew what a factory was really like, "one remained stupefied by the tiny rapport between the daily life of workers and the debates of their own organization." Accordingly she made all sorts of proposals (regarding obligatory arbitration, cadence work, union input into the problem of balancing fatigue against a reasonable productive level, and various means of defending worker dignity through workers' control), but to little avail.[42] This too, then, reinforced her view that the problem of workers' liberation was far more complicated than "which side came out on top." Even the leaders of workers' organizations were relatively insensitive to the dimensions of the oppression which workers faced in the modern age.

One of Simone Weil's most troubling realizations while working at the Renault factory was that her own feeling of slavery deepened. She remarked that at the time she could have been told to get off a bus without any reason and would have obeyed without a murmur, finding this the most natural thing in the world. She noted that her sense of being a slave made her completely lose the feeling of having any rights.[43] Periods when she did not have to bear with any brutality became like gifts of fortune for her.[44] Thus she concluded (in contrast to the sanguine rhetoric of the Marxists of her generation) that workers were no more likely to rebel against their oppressors than slaves would inevitably rise up and overthrow their tyrannical masters: ". . . an obviously inexorable and invincible oppression does not engender

---

40 Cf. Ibid., 52, 55, 60.
41 Letter to Nicholas Lazarévitch. Cited in Pétrement, *Weil*, 2: 34. Weil was not alone in this sentiment. The French Communist Party in this period also denounced the "fascist Plan of the C.G.T."
42 Cf. Simone Weil, "Le Congrès des Métaux," *Le Libertaire* (December 4, 1936). Cited in Pétrement, *Weil*, 2: 116.
43 Weil, *La Condition*, 124.
44 Weil, *Waiting for God*, 33.

revolt as an immediate reaction, but rather submission."[45] Weil's loss of faith in the old revolutionary premise that oppression necessarily engendered revolt had an important influence on her subsequent intellectual and spiritual evolution, as we shall see. Decades before Alexander Solzhenitsyn would illustrate this same fact of the human condition with great power in his novels and chronicles of his own experience of prison life, Weil perceived the brutalizing effects of the worst of modern factory work. Her revelations, like those of Solzhenitsyn, had to serve as warning to revolutionaries with an optimistic faith in the possibility of revolutions necessarily bringing liberty in their wake, or who were blindly optimistic about liberty in general.

The pessimism underlying Simone Weil's observations of the industrial world by no means caused her to abandon all attempts to engender rebellion among its "slaves." Her factory experience did, however, influence her reflections about what and how something could be done about the more oppressive features of modern society. On the one hand, when requested to do so, she formulated some practical proposals. In a proposal somewhat similar to what Charles de Gaulle would call "participation," she proposed that factory workers and management exchange views: the workers would propose ameliorations in their condition to their bosses; the bosses would, in turn, explain why certain reforms were difficult or impossible. If workers' claims were not met, she suggested passive disobedience, whether the state be capitalist or "socialist." On the other hand, her factory experience led her to broaden the scope of her reflections even further beyond traditional political and social channels.

The factory experience greatly increased Weil's scepticism about the ability, or even the will, of the elites of modern industrial societies to come to grips with the problems of the working class. This was not a matter of ideologies, nor even of the level of technical progress; it had to do with the most basic mechanisms of modern industrial society and the modern scientific culture in both the West and the East. She concluded that workers simply had to be sceptical of intellectuals and technicians, whatever their intentions, belief-systems, politics or rhetoric. Capitalist industrialists could always subsidize, or totalitarian states promote, technical experts who would seek to have "scientific rules" applied to the workers. But workers, she thought, should never have confidence in technicians or intellectuals regulating matters of vital importance to themselves.[46]

---

45 Weil, La Condition, 145.
46 Cf. "La Rationalisation" (February 23, 1937) in La Condition, 289-315 and especially 314-15.

Not long after her practical foray, Simone Weil attended Charlie Chaplin's *Modern Times* with one of her students and remarked cryptically that only *Charlot* really understood the condition of the worker in our time.[47] Soon afterward she would conclude that Jesus, too, had understood some things better than Trotsky or Marx.

It was Simone Weil's scepticism about the efficacy of revolutionary initiatives to respond to workers' problems that eventually stimulated her more profound and wide-ranging inquiries about the underpinnings of the technological society. Her precocious analysis of the beliefs which inspired the myth of progress, in turn, led her to conclude that most political responses to the most serious problems of the modern world were woefully narrow in focus. The more she sought to grasp the most profound forces shaping modern Western society, and adequate remedies for those she considered noxious, the more she became interested in religious responses to, and explanations of, reality.

47 Pétrement, *Weil*, 2: 96.

3
PATRIOTISM AND HITLER

Is God French?

The cult of Joan of Arc, originally promoted by the eccentric sculptor Real del Sarte, but taken over and expanded by the Action Française, symbolized the fusion of nationalistic sentiment and religious fervour in early twentieth century France.[1] Simone Weil, too, belongs within the distinctive "Renaissance" of religious thought and literature which was a remarkable feature of France in the first half of this century: despite her undoubted genius and originality it is certain that we would have had a very different Simone Weil had she not been able to share her metaphysical and spiritual concerns with men such as Father Perrin, Gustave Thibon, and Georges Bernanos. But in some extremely important ways, Simone Weil was on the "other side" with regard to the Catholic intellectuals with whom she so often associated. One important reason for that was her unfashionable attitude toward French nationalism.

Some of the most eloquent writings which the Catholic revival produced were on the special destiny of France. Not only the more "pagan" nationalists such as Maurras and Barrès, but deeply serious Christians such as Bernanos, Léon Bloy, Paul Claudel, and the young Jacques Maritain believed in a special relationship between their

---

1 Cf. Ernst Nolte, "The Action Française," in his *Three Faces of Fascism* (New York, 1966), 29-141.

37

beloved country and Divine Providence.[2] And this group was not exclusively right-wing; perhaps the most powerful poetry with this inspiration flowed from the pen of the Dreyfusard, socialist, and Catholic, Charles Péguy. Not only did he produce the most impressive celebration of Joan of Arc's special meaning for France, and France's special calling to the world, but he went so far as to describe God Himself as French ("'Je suis bon Français,' dit Dieu"). France, for Péguy, represented civilization, Christianity itself. He went off to his early death, into the slaughter of World War I, with a joy in his heart. One recalls his famous lines: "Heureux ceux qui sont morts dans les grandes batailles / Couchés dessus le sol à la face de Dieu."[3]

Péguy's fusing of Christian and patriotic sentiment was still more distasteful to Simone Weil than the relatively simplistic chauvinism of a Charles Maurras or Maurice Barrès. The latter, for her, was merely brutal and primitive, while Péguyiste patriotic Catholicism was blasphemous, an insult to God himself, which she saw as a ruder perversion of the modern Western religious consciousness. Writing with the free French in London during the war, for the eyes of De Gaulle (who had been raised with precisely the Catholic-nationalist mentality she detested), Simone Weil directly challenged not only an important element of the Resistance spirit, but also one of the presuppositions of a man like the General:

> It was the fashion before 1940 to talk about "eternal France." Such words are a sort of blasphemy. One is compelled to say the same about the many pages which have been written by great French Catholic writers on the vocation of France, the eternal salvation of France, and similar themes.[4]

For Weil such sentiments were not only windy exaggerations. She raised serious questions about the way in which many French Christians—of the Right and of the Left, of Vichy as well as of the Resistance—saw the place of their nation within their total view of the universe. She attacked the very basis for a "religious" nationalism: "France is something which is temporal, terrestrial. Unless I am mistaken, it has never been suggested that Christ died to save nations. The idea of a nation being chosen by God for itself simply belongs to

2 A very interesting recent analysis of this phenomenon is contained in Richard Griffiths, The Reactionary Revolution: The Catholic Revival in French Literature, 1870-1914 (London, 1966).
3 "Blessed are those who died in great battles / Lying on the ground in the sight of God" (from the poem Eve [Paris, 1913]).
4 Weil, The Need for Roots, translated by Arthur Wills (New York, 1971), 131.

the old Mosaic law." And, in the specific case of France, she dared to raise questions about the national saint of France herself: "Joan of Arc's popularity during the past quarter of a century was not an altogether healthy business; it was a convenient way of forgetting that there is a difference between France and God."[5]

Thus Simone Weil raised fundamental questions about the way in which many of her compatriots unreflectively fused their feelings toward their suffering nation and the Creator. Was France indeed "eternal," part of God's plan for all of human history? Could one say with any assurance that one of the reasons for Christ's sacrifice was to preserve the French nation? For some Frenchmen, Joan of Arc resolved all of this because she was obviously called by God to save France. But Simone Weil asked if the popular veneration of Joan of Arc was properly focussed. Were Frenchmen clear-eyed about the sort of patriotism which the soldier-saint displayed, and its relationship to the teachings of Jesus.

During the Second World War Christians of opposing nations confronted and killed one another across the battle lines of Europe in the sincere belief that their own nation's cause was one with God's. Simone Weil, coming to the Christian religion from the outside, met this terrible paradox head on. She found that the question of the relationship between God and particular nations is one on which believers in the Western religious traditions have not been particularly well versed.

In surveying the Western historical tradition she found that the notion of a people or nation being specially chosen for a God-given destiny was mercifully absent from pagan antiquity. True, she granted, the Romans considered themselves as "specially chosen"—"but solely for world dominion. They were not concerned with the next world." Nowhere else, she charged, was there any people or city who thought themselves chosen for a "supernatural destiny."[6] Of course when she wrote this Simone Weil was living among Frenchmen in London, many of whom were firmly convinced that their cause was that of France, and the cause of France was the one most favoured by God. But Simone Weil was too sober not to see the paradox in the heavy religious rhetoric of Vichy, or, for that matter, in that of the German enemy. If some peoples, like the Americans, were particularly ostentatious in their conviction that God favoured their nation, this cast of mind was found on all sides in the European conflict.

5 Ibid., 132-33.
6 Ibid., 131.

How did the different Western nations come to accept that their particular country or people was favoured of God? Here Simone Weil rejected the contention that this was an ancient pagan notion reappearing in modern guise (i.e., the old cliché: modern nationalism is a reappearance of the old pagan idolatry of the state). In fact, she argued, this "mistake" was not at all common in pre-Christian antiquity. When a tendency to recognize only collective values appeared in antiquity it was among the Romans, who were atheists, and the Hebrews—but only up to their Babylonian exile. Thus, for her, the modern tendency to revive this error was due to the corruption exercised by an aberrant dual Roman-Hebrew tradition. Christians had to recognize that this ran directly up against the pure Christian inspiration on this question.[7]

Of course it would be easy for French Christians of the Resistance to argue that their motivation and patriotism was more purely Christian than that of, for example, the Germans—whose Nazis were obviously more pagan in style. But she refused to see this issue as a question of degree. It was a question of fundamentals:

> Christians today don't like raising the question of the respective rights over their heart enjoyed by God and their country. The German bishops ended one of their most courageous protests by saying that they refused ever to have to make a choice between God and Germany. And why did they refuse to do this? Circumstances can always arise which make it necessary to choose between God and no matter what earthly object, and the choice must never be in doubt. But the French bishops would not have expressed themselves any differently.[8]

Why was Simone Weil's rejection of "religious" nationalism so uncompromising? Behind it were her perceptions of the impurities in modern Western spirituality, as well as her understanding of the subtler roots of both fascism and Stalinism. Here again her ideas were original and unsettling for many of her contemporaries as she suggested the way of resistance to fascism was not as simple, or as easy on the conscience, as many of her fellows-in-arms seemed to think. "Fascism," she charged, was "always intimately connected with a certain variety of patriotic feeling."[9]

---

7   Ibid., 132. There is, of course, an analogous tension in Marxism, with international "pure" Marxism and nationalist-Marxist regimes of all sorts.
8   Ibid., 132-33.
9   Ibid., 148.

On Patriotism: False and True

There was, warned Simone Weil in London during the war, a very serious "confusion of thought and feeling over the subject of patriotism."[10] Since, as De Gaulle's *Mémoires de Guerre* would so eloquently attest, a sense of French patriotism and honour were a vital source of inspiration for the Resistance this was a curious time and context to be making such a charge. But, with her habitual faculty for getting to the bottom of things, Weil sought to examine the soundness of the Resistance inspiration and the efficacy and breadth of its rejection of fascism. She wanted to know if the superiority of the resisters' motivations was as self-evident as one liked to assume.

If French resisters could admire the "grandeur," the "heroic glamour" of France at the apex of her power under Richelieu, or Louis XIV, could not contemporary Germany also attract similar approval? German soldiers in World War II could surely be "heroes" for someone in the same way as were those of the all-powerful Sun King. If the resisters objected that the French soldiers then, and now, were fighting with a more noble inspiration than that of the enemy, Simone Weil did not see it: "Is there any guarantee at all that a French soldier in Africa is inspired by a purer ideal of sacrifice than that of a German soldier in Russia? Actually, there isn't any."[11] For her, then, there was an implicit weakness in the Resistance insofar as it combatted the Nazis in the name of notions such as the supernatural destiny of "eternal France," or out of a sense of offended national honour or "grandeur," or out of an admiration for heroism, and contempt for cowardice. She suggested that none of these inspirations was what profound resistance to fascism required—precisely because all such noble notions shared, to a lesser or greater degree, in the basic impulses behind the phenomenon of Hitlerism itself.

If so much patriotism was perverse and deformed, what kind was legitimate and justifiable? And what sort of feeling could inspire it? Simone Weil argued that there was a feeling "no less vital, absolutely pure, and corresponding exactly to the present circumstances": compassion for a country. As if to give the lie to the super-patriot Catholics she returned to the figure of Joan of Arc as a "glorious respondent"; the maid of Orleans, Weil recalled, rather than trumpeting France's glories, said she "felt pity for the Kingdom of France." Compassion for one's country, Weil insisted, did not exclude warlike energy. But it was a far more noble sentiment than the ones evoked earlier. She described it as a "purer" patriotism, inspired by love:

10 Ibid., 170.
11 Ibid.

> A perfectly pure love for one's country bears a close resemblance to the feelings which his young children, his aged parents, or a beloved wife inspire in a man. The thought of weakness can inflame love in just the same way as can the thought of strength, but in the former case the flame is of an altogether different order of purity.[12]

The focus and style of this love of country was antithetical to the trumpeting patriotism of the fascists, and should inspire the true attitude of resistance.

It is clear that Simone Weil's standard of patriotism not only set her over against the fascists, but separated her from the great leaders of the French resistance as well. The contrast between her view and that of Charles de Gaulle is, again, most striking. For de Gaulle, France was indeed "eternal" and could never be truncated and absorbed into a Hitlerite Europe. And beyond that, French honour and France's glory as a great nation-state demanded fidelity, a spirit of self-sacrifice and love. For Simone Weil, however, such patriotism was misplaced and shared in some of the worst vices of the enemy. The sort of compassion for one's country which she demanded was different from the sense of tradition and pride of De Gaulle: "This poignantly tender feeling for some beautiful, fragile and perishable object has a warmth about it which the sentiment of national grandeur altogether lacks."[13] Thus, for her, the alternatives facing the Resistance were even sharper than any of her compatriots seemed to imagine. It was even more important to be sensitive to the vices of the fascists than most members of the Resistance seemed to realize.

Simone Weil foresaw two divergent paths for the French Resistance, only one of which would purge her country of the false patriotism which had so much damaged the West: "One can either love France for the glory which would seem to ensure for her a prolonged existence in time and space; or else one can love her as something which, being earthly, can be destroyed, and is all the more precious on that account."[14] For Simone Weil these represented two distinct ways of loving, and two distinct kinds of patriotism. The "compassionate" sort described above was the only one which she saw as legitimate for a Christian. Her notion of love of country, inspired by charity rather than chest-thumping pride, certainly challenged the beliefs of many of her contemporaries in many countries and on all points along the political spectrum. We shall see that she was quick to support it with far ranging historical argumentation.

12 Ibid., 172
13 Ibid., 171.
14 Ibid., 172.

While still a student, Simone Weil had believed that the Communists had a far sounder attitude toward the nation than had the Right. But her first hand observations of the peculiar "nationalism" of the proletariat was sobering. First of all, in the Spanish Civil War, she had been shocked by the cruelty and brutality exercised by working class Republicans against enemies whom they had classified into enemy "nations" of all sorts—"fascists," "Italians," "priests."[15] Then, years later, she had the disillusioning experience of observing Sovietophile French workers calculating the Front line losses of the allies from a notice board: their indifference to the figures of the British dead was in sharp contrast to their quick sorrow at Soviet losses. Their sentiment of solidarity with the international proletariat counted for little against their Communist solidarity with Russia, fatherland of the working class. Despite all of the Marxist rhetoric, Stalinism simply encouraged this left-wing variety of nationalism among French workers: "A huge, powerful, sovereign state, governing a territory much vaster than that of their own country says to them, 'I am yours . . . . I exist only to serve you, and before long I will make you undisputed masters in your own country.' "[16]

Thus the "internationalism" of the Stalinist-influenced working class was illusory in the experience of Simone Weil. Instead of present day Communism offering an alternative to the militant nationalism which divided Europe, it set up an "idolatry" of its own. If the Resistance could not inspire the people of France with the kind of pure love of country she recommended, she warned that they would fall into the "Communist idolatry" of the Stalinists, or their idolatry could take the nationalist form of having as its object "the pair of idols so characteristic of our age": the Leader and the State. The fostering of true patriotism demanded a complete purification of feeling.

Hitler, the New Caesar

Simone Weil had been struck by the base cruelty of the anarchist leader Durruti who had captured a fifteen-year-old Falangist wearing a religious medal. Durruti had given him twenty-four hours to decide to switch sides and then had him shot dead when he had refused.[17] The French Catholic novelist Bernanos, who had sympathized with the other side in the conflict until he observed, first

15 See her letter to Georges Bernanos in Weil, *Ecrits historiques et politiques* (Paris, 1960), 221-22.
16 Weil, *Roots*, 153.
17 Weil, *Ecrits historiques*, 221-22.

hand, their brutality in Majorca, won the admiration of Simone Weil for his book *Les grands cimetières sous la lune*[18] in which the savagery of both sides is denounced. Like Georges Bernanos, she was working toward a total, radical renunciation of the profoundest roots of fascism. Thus she was impressed by Bernanos' analysis of the nature of Hitlerism which he described as basically a return to pagan Rome.

It was fashionable for the French (and Westerners in general) to attribute the phenomenon of Hitlerism to German national peculiarities, to a mysterious movement called Nazism, or to the evil genius of Adolf Hitler. This was far less demanding and more comfortable than any self-scrutiny to discern traces of the origins of Hitlerism in oneself. And this is precisely what Simone Weil required. Her insistence was that the Roman impulse lay at Hitlerism's root cause and that Rome not only influenced the Nazis but played and plays an extremely influential part in the history, culture, and everyday thoughts of the entire West.

Simone Weil stressed that Hitler had been profoundly influenced in his youth by a mediocre book on the Roman tyrant Sulla. For her, Hitler achieved exactly the sort of greatness which was depicted in that book, and it was the very sort for which the modern West retained "a servile admiration." It was impossible to punish Hitler because he desired one thing alone, and he achieved it: to play a part in history. For Hitler, an "idolater of history," "everything connected with history must be good."[19] Thus, whatever Hitler was made to suffer could not stop him from feeling himself to be a great man. Beyond that, the emergence of future Hitlers (always a possibility as long as an admiration for the values represented by Hitler persisted) would not be forestalled by Hitler's punishment either: " . . . it will not stop, in twenty, fifty, a hundred or two hundred year's time, some solitary little dreamer, whether German or otherwise, from seeing in Hitler a superb figure, with a superb destiny from beginning to end, and desiring with all his soul to have a similar destiny. In which case, woe betide his contemporaries."[20]

There was only one way of giving Hitler his just desserts, according to Simone Weil, and it demanded a fundamental and difficult shift in mentality in Western culture. Again her analysis is unique:

> The only punishment capable of punishing Hitler, and deterring
> little boys thirsting for greatness in coming centuries from follow-

18 Georges Bernanos, *Les grands cimetières sous la lune* (Paris, 1938).
19 Here Weil anticipates Karl Popper's *The Open Society and Its Enemies*, 2 vols. (London, 1945).
20 Weil, *Roots*, 227.

ing his example is such a total transformation of the meaning attached to greatness that he should thereby be excluded from it. It is chimerical and due to the blindness induced by national hatred to imagine that one can exclude Hitler from the title to greatness without a total transformation, among the men of today, of the idea and significance of greatness.[21]

As long as Hitler was considered merely a psychopathic personality, or the sort of leader who could only emerge among "The Hun," Hitler was being addressed from a "superior" position which was, in fact, not entirely dissimilar from that which Hitler maintained. But if, as Simone Weil insisted, Hitler was not an incongruous and alien figure but a reincarnation of a persistent Western phenomenon—from Sulla through Napoleon—then a more profound and wide-ranging remedy for Hitlerism was necessary.

The purgation of Hitlerism was up to each individual to accomplish inside his own mind. It entailed consciously "modifying the scope of the sentiment attached to greatness." This she agreed was extremely difficult, since there was immense social pressure opposed to such a radical conversion of values. She even argued that "to be able to carry it out, one has to exclude oneself spiritually from the rest of society."[22] Simone Weil certainly excluded herself spiritually from the rest of society to accomplish this conversion personally. And here she was inspired by the example of great religious figures who also took radical departure from the accepted notions of power and glory in their days.

Simone Weil's attachment to the teachings of Jesus must be linked with her effort to understand, and resist, Hitlerism. Since she was particularly sensitive to the "Roman" element in Nazism she paid special attention to Christ's attitude toward the basic values of the empire in which he lived. Here she was struck by the way Jesus embodied an anti-Roman, anti-imperialist outlook which ran directly against the perverted nationalism and patriotisms she loathed. He had displayed a kind of pure love of country that she could admire:

> In the Gospels there is not the least indication that Christ experienced anything resembling love for Jerusalem and Judea, save only the love which goes wrapped in compassion. He never showed any other kind of attachment to his country ... [than] the compassion He expressed on more than one occasion. He wept over the city, foreseeing ... the destruction which should shortly fall upon it.[23]

21 Ibid.
22 Ibid.
23 Ibid., 170.

Perhaps Simone Weil was the first ever to propose Jesus as the best model for patriotism and "nationalism." But it is clear that her interpretation afforded precisely the antithesis to fascism, and an antidote to Hitler, which she had sought. For her, the compassionate teachings of Christ represented a "light of justice" in Western man's historical experience. Over against that was the value system which, in the long view, nurtured fascism: "Below comes the darkness in which the strong sincerely believe that their cause is more just than that of the weak. That was the case with the Romans and the Hebrews."[24] Thus a distinctive perspective of Western history emerged behind Simone Weil's critique of the scourges of fascism and nationalism. The Nazis were not such an unprecedented aberration as many of their enemies found comfortable to believe. The Nazis' self-righteous contempt for the weak had been presaged by other peoples, other periods in the West, and among them were the Romans and ancient Hebrews who—ironical as it may seem in an age afflicted with Nazism—were still admired.

For Simone Weil, Western history was "a tissue of base and cruel acts," a story of cruelty and brutality, from the Romans through the Stalinists and Nazis. Christ's teachings had represented a counter-force. This unusual view of the historical drama of the West led her to work out her own, very original philosophy of history.

24 Weil, "Forms of the Implicit Love of God," in *Waiting for God*, translated by Emma Craufurd (London, 1950), 99.

4

HISTORY, THE OLD TESTAMENT, AND ROMAN TRADITION

The Jehovah of the Bible versus the Father of the Gospels

Friedrich Nietzsche told the story of the decline of the God-type: from the National Warrior-God of the early Hebrews to the God of the nooks and crannies, the "Spider-God," of the Christians:

> Formerly he represented a people, the strength of a people, everything aggressive and thirsting for power in the soul of a people: now he is merely the good God.... How can one today ... join ... in proclaiming that the evolution of the concept of God from the "God of Israel," the national God, to the Christian God, the epitome of everything good, is an *advance?*... When the prerequisites of *ascending* life, when everything strong, brave, masterful, proud is eliminated from the concept of God; when he declines step by step ... when he becomes the poor people's God, the sinner's God, the God of the sick *par excellence* ... of *what* does such a transformation speak? Such a *reduction* of the divine?[1]

Simone Weil's view, totally antithetical to that of the author of *The Anti-Christ*, was that the Hebrews, up until the Babylonian exile,

---

1 F. W. Nietzsche, *The Twilight of the Idols and the Anti-Christ*, translated by R. J. Hollingdale (Middlesex, 1968), 126.

47

had an undeveloped religious sensibility, and were—like the Romans—"only capable of recognizing collective values" and ready to proclaim the righteousness of a victory of the strong over the weak. It was only gradually, according to her, that the Hebrews began to transcend their brutal and racialist qualities and evolve toward the values taught by the later prophets, and then, with such clarity, by Jesus. For her, a thorough critique of the roots of fascist and Stalinist impulses required at least as severe an evaluation of the Jewish tradition as it did of European nationalism and Christian idolatries.

Since she was raised with little formation in her own Jewish religious heritage Simone Weil's first reservations about the Old Testament seem to have been provoked when, in her later religious phase, she turned toward reading it with her "outsider's" perspective. She was particularly shocked by two stories, one relating to God's order to Saul, the other concerning the prophet Elijah. According to 1 Samuel 15, God ordered King Saul to slay the Amalekites "both men and women, infant and suckling, ox and sheep, camel and ass." She asked: Could God give such an order? Why had neither the Bible writer nor later Christians raised this issue? And then in 2 Kings 2:23-24 we are told that Elijah was on his way to Bethel when a large group of children mocked him. He cursed them, and two she-bears emerged from a wood and devoured forty-two of them. For Weil this put not only Elijah but the whole Old Testament idea of God in question: by His atrocious miracle God seemed to approve Elijah's curse.[2] Of course children raised within the Biblical tradition learn to consider the enemies of Israel and the prophets as wicked. Simone Weil, reading the Scriptures for the first time in her late twenties, raised new questions about the relationship of the Bible to the inhuman phenomena of the twentieth century.

After a few years of study and reflection on the matter of the Old Testament, Simone Weil's ideas became more precise. She came to admire certain psalms, the Song of Songs, Isaiah, Daniel, and, above all, the book of Job. But she was confirmed in her feeling that the early Hebrews were religious primitives and their sense of God was relatively savage in comparison with many of their neighbours. That Westerners raised with the Bible had learned to consider the people who had surrounded the early Jews as polytheistic "idolators" she considered a falsehood ascribable to Jewish fanaticism: in fact "All peoples of all ages have always been monotheistic."[3] At the beginning, she thought, "Israel, which lacked a revelation, was very much

2 Pétrement, Weil, 2: 217-18.
3 Weil, Letter to a Priest," in Gateway, 105.

inferior to all those so-called idolatries."[4] The Bible showed that
"There was very little spirituality in Israel until the Exile."[5] The
experience of the Israelites in Egypt had left them untouched by faith
"in immortality, in salvation, in the fusion of the soul with God
through Charity," all of which existed in Egypt.[6] Moses had been
initiated into the wisdom of the Egyptian priests but he had "refused
that wisdom, because like Maurras, he thought of religion as a simple
instrument of national grandeur."[7]

Thus, like Nietzsche, Simone Weil saw a link between the sense
of God and the sense of national pride and vitality of the ancient
Hebrews. But while Nietzsche had seen the relationship between the
nation and God as "correct" among the virile and warlike ancient
Hebrews, and then entering on a period of gradual decline toward the
sheepish religion of Jesus, Simone Weil saw the early Jewish religious
sensibility as unpraiseworthy:

> If we take a moment in history anterior to Christ and sufficiently
> remote from Him—for example, five centuries before His time—and
> we set aside what follows afterwards, at that moment Israel has less
> of a share in God and in divine truth than several of the surrounding
> peoples (India, Egypt, Greece, China). For the essential truth con-
> cerning God is that he is good. To believe that God can order men to
> commit atrocious acts of injustice and cruelty is the greatest mistake
> it is possible to make with regard to Him.[8]

Thus Weil thought that all of the Old Testament—apart from the
few texts she cited and explained as exceptions—fell into this "fundamental error concerning God." And those few texts that were exceptions led her to think that Israel had not been at the most advanced
edge of religious perceptions, as has often been assumed, but rather
"Israel learnt the most essential truth about God (i.e., that God is good
before being powerful) from foreign traditional sources: Chaldean,
Persian, or Greek, and thanks to the exile."[9] As for the Scriptural
denunciations of the idolatry of neighbouring peoples, she ascribed
them to "Jewish fanaticism" and suggested what such a perspective
would mean in the contemporary world:

> If some Hebrews of classical Jewry were to return to life and were to
> be provided with arms, they would exterminate the lot of us—men,

4 Weil, Cahiers (Paris, 1974), 3: 221.
5 Weil, Intuitions pré-chrétiennes (Paris, 1951), 110.
6 Weil, La Connaissance surnaturelle (Paris, 1950), 212.
7 Weil, Letter to Jean Wahl. Cited in Pétrement, Weil, 2: 447.
8 "Letter to a Priest," in Gateway, 105.
9 Ibid., 106.

women, and children, for the crime of idolatry. They would re-
proach us for worshipping Baal and Astarte, taking Christ for Baal
and the Virgin for Astarte.[10]

For her, this self-righteous brutality against "idolatrous" neighbours
was ironic because the Hebrews themselves were idolators. Veritable
idolatry, she argued, was covetousness; and "the Jewish nation, in its
thirst for carnal good, was guilty of this in the very moments, even
when it was worshipping its God." This idolatry of the Jewish
nation was of a kind she found particularly pernicious: "The Hebrews took for their idol, not something made of metal or wood, but a
race, a nation, something just as earthly. Their religion is
essentially inseparable from such idolatry, because of the notion of
the 'chosen people.' "[11] Thus, for her, the Old Testament perception
of God with the cruelties of the Jehovah described therein, the nationalism of the Hebrews, and their condemnation of the "idolatries"
of their neighbours, were all of a piece. And coming to Christianity
from the outside as she was, she wondered that more had not been
made in the past of the contradictions between the harshness of the
Old Testament and the gentleness of the New, the cruelty of Jehovah
and the gentleness of Jesus. After applying herself to the study of these
matters she wrote to historian of religion, Déodat Roché: "I have never
been able to understand how it is possible for a reasonable mind to
regard the Jehovah of the Bible and the Father who is invoked in the
Gospel as one and the same being."[12]

Nietzsche, one assumes, would have agreed with this, as he was
sensitive to precisely the same tension. The analyses of Nietzsche and
those of Weil on the contrasts and contradiction between the Old and
the New Testaments are often parallel. But the side Simone Weil took
in all of this was the obverse—thus her distinctive view of Western
history, Christianity, and the origins of racism and nationalism.

Nietzsche's notion of the decline of the "God-type" in the West
gave him a distinctive understanding of the "ups and downs" of the
Western historical experience. The periods or cultures he admired
were those in which men displayed "healthy" religious perceptions
like those of the ancient Hebrews—or enjoyed a frankly pagan celebration of life, devoid of a sense of God. Thus he had special admiration for the ancient Greeks (before the "decadence" of Socrates and

10 Ibid.
11 Ibid., 107.
12 "Letter to Déodat Roché" (January 23, 1940) published in Weil, *Pensées sans ordre
    concernant l'amour de Dieu* (Paris, 1962), and in *The Simone Weil Reader*, edited
    by George Panichas (New York, 1968), 83.

Plato), for the *Imperium Romanum* (before the "sickness" of Christianity), for the mature Italian Renaissance (before the simple-minded "rebellion" of the Reformation), for the France of Louis XIV and Bossuet (struggling against the influence of the "sublime misanthrope" Pascal and the Jansenists), and for the nobility of Napoleon (insofar as he put down the herd instincts inspired in the *canaille* by Rousseau and the French Revolution). Nietzsche, despite his contempt for Christianity, made an exception in his admiration for the Roman Catholic Church—particularly for its periods (the Renaissance) or institutions (the Jesuits) which did most to suppress the "poison" of the Gospels. He particularly loathed the "evil eye for the world," the life denying aspects, of the New Testament, and harboured a special disdain for those ages, cultures, or individuals who displayed these qualities with the most prominence.

Simone Weil's evaluation of Western history began with totally different moral premises and reached precisely the opposite conclusions. For the most part, she reviled the ages and individuals Nietzsche admired and appreciated those for which he had the most contempt. Her view of history was that of an inverted "overman," and certainly no less radical and original.

The rejection of Old Testament cruelty and nationalism was at the basis of the understanding of history which Simone Weil worked out. From the time of her original religious reflections about the Old Testament, she developed a sympathetic interest in the second century teachings of Marcion, foe of Tertullian.[13] The extreme gnosticism of Marcion pictured not only a difference, but a struggle, between the God of the Old Testament and that of the Gospels. Thus, unlike Nietzsche, she hailed the emergence of the Christian God as a sign of great spiritual evolution and progress over the Old Testament Jehovah whom Nietzsche—and Marcion's opponent Tertullian—admired. And so the subsequent centuries of the West presented a series of "ups and downs" according to whether or not the "pure" spirit of Christianity, or a return to paganism and savagery prevailed. She reserved her greatest admiration for the periods and peoples that Nietzsche condemned as "life-denying": for the stoics, the early Christians, for the Cathars (the "pure"—an eleventh century neo-platonic sect that reacted strongly against the authoritarianism of the Church and re-

13 Cf. Pétrement, *Weil*, 2: 218, 402. Marcion (A.D. 140) was a wealthy shipowner of Sinope and Rome who converted to Christianity while insisting on the great contrast between the God of the Old Testament and that of the New. He regarded Paul as the foremost interpreter of Christian doctrine and set up his own Church, based on democratic tenets, and regarded the ascetic life and celibacy as the ideal existence.

jected most of the Old Testament with the exception of the Prophets, the psalms, and the Books of Wisdom). She also admired the Christian humanism of the early Renaissance. It was her distinctive view that the true Christian spirit was husbanded in this milieu—among the gnostics and manicheans—in the course of Western history and that the trends admired by Nietzsche were the faith's enemies. Here, one assumes, Nietzsche would be in full agreement.

Rome: The "Great Beast of the Apocalypse"

In the same letter in which she confessed to the expert on the Cathars (Déodat Roché) her own problem in reconciling the Jehovah of the Bible and the Father of the New Testament, Weil suggested her perspective on the spiritual evolution of the West:

> The influence of the Old Testament and of the Roman Empire, whose tradition was continued by the Papacy, are to my mind the two essential sources of the corruption of Christianity.
> ... coarseness of mind and baseness of heart ... were disseminated over vast territories by the Roman domination and ... still, today, compose the atmosphere of Europe.[14]

Weil has often been accused of excessive harshness in her criticism of ancient Israel. But in fact her distaste for the Roman Empire was even more extreme, and essential to her understanding of history and what she perceived to be the "rootlessness" of the modern world. She argued that the empire of the Romans (which Nietzsche so admired) was one of the worst historical misfortunes besetting mankind before the Nazis:

> From the point of view of the development of humanity, the Roman Empire is the deadliest phenomenon to be found in history. It killed and even destroyed all trace of several civilizations and it put an end to that whole prodigious commerce of ideas in the Mediterranean basin, which made the grandeur of what we call antiquity.[15]

The Roman Empire was essentially destructive and not, as Nietzsche had thought, the pinnacle of human achievement.[16] Her horror at the pernicious influence of Rome was not only based upon its ruinous effect on the cultures of antiquity which she admired, but also on its

14 Weil, "Letter to Déodat Roché, in *Weil Reader*, 83.
15 Weil, *Selected Essays, 1934-1943*, translated by Richard Rees (New York, 1962), 76.
16 This is the popular, if perhaps unfair, view on Nietzsche and the Romans.

subsequent corrupting influence on Christianity and the whole of Western culture—through Hitlerism. The Roman Empire for her was not only a historical phenomenon for scholars to assess, whose merits could be debated fifteen hundred years later. It was, particularly in its long relationship with the Christian Church, a nefarious cosmological presence described in the more prophetic works of the Gospels: "And in what circumstances was accomplished the collusion between the Church of Christ and the Beast? For the Beast of the Apocalypse is almost certainly the Empire."[17] Thus in her view the iniquitous Empire complemented the idolatry of Israel to form the curse of Western history: "Rome is the Great Beast of atheism and materialism, adoring nothing but itself. Israel is the great beast of religion. Neither the one nor the other is likeable. The Great Beast is always repulsive."[18]

How was Rome the malefic force in antiquity described by the Gospel writer? Simone Weil laid a whole range of charges against the Empire. For her, Roman imperialism—with its aggressive atheism and materialism—destroyed the spiritual milieu which originally gave birth to Christianity. It uprooted and enslaved its neighbours, introduced a pernicious form of patriotism and slavery, and then debased and corrupted Christianity itself—unto the Christians' very sense of God. Thus she saw the twin poisons of Jewish nationalist idolatry and Roman brutality creating the special atmosphere necessary for the drama of Jesus' death: "Such a horrible thing as the crucifixion of Christ could only happen in a place in which evil far outweighed good. But not only that, the Church born and bred in such a place must needs be impure from the beginning."[19] For Weil, then, the essence of Jesus' teachings, born in antiquity, ran directly against the spirit of the Jews and the whole value system of the Romans. The tragedy was that the Christian Church was profoundly reshaped by these peoples who represented its antithesis. Christianity underwent a "double defilement" which "explains all the subsequent defilements that made the history of the Church such an atrocious one across the centuries": Israel caused the Old Testament to be accepted by Christianity as a sacred book; Rome turned Christianity into the official religion of the Roman Empire.[20]

This notion that the whole history of the Church has been terribly and tragically marked by double influences of Israel and Rome was responsible for much that was original and unique in Simone Weil's

---

17 Weil, "Letter to a Priest," in *Gateway*, 143.
18 Weil, The Great Beast," in *Weil Reader*, 393.
19 Weil, "Letter to a Priest," in *Gateway*, 123.
20 Ibid.

view of history. She wondered over the fate of "pure" Christianity, its sources and its legacy. This led to her interest in the Albigensian heresy and the culture and spirituality of the Cathars, which afforded her a great revelation. She found the Albigensians a pinnacle of human spiritual achievement (comparable to the Romans for Nietzsche). First of all they were a remarkably artistically and intellectually productive people. She thought that "French thought has been more enriched by the Albigenses and troubadors of the twelfth century . . . than by the entire output from this part of France in the course of succeeding centuries."[21] But even apart from their intellectual and artistic achievements, she found the Cathars remarkable for the quality of their religiosity. It helped confirm her important conclusion about the origins of Christianity, reinforced by extensive study in Patristic literature and ancient religions, that the authentic spirit of Christianity owed far more to the ancient cultures of the Near East and Mediterranean areas than to the Jews and to Rome, as Christians usually assumed. She wrote of her new insight to the authority on the Cathars, Roché, in January 1940:

> Your studies have confirmed a thought of mine which I already had before reading them. It is that Catharism was the last living expression in Europe of pre-Roman antiquity. I believe that before the conquests of Rome the countries of the Mediterranean and the Near East formed a civilization, which was not homogeneous, because it varied greatly from one country to another, but was continuous; and I believe that one and the same thought inhabited all its best minds and was expressed in various forms in the mysteries and the initiatory sects of Egypt, Thrace, Greece, and Persia, and that the works of Plato are the most perfect written expression which we possess of that thought. . . . It is from this thought that Christianity issued; but only the Gnostics, Manichaeans, and Cathars seem to have kept really faithful to it.[22]

Weil told Roché that she thought that the scarcity of texts made it impossible to prove her theory.[23] But subsequently she made a significant effort to do just that in late 1941 and early 1942 when, after a study of Greek thought with Father Perrin, she decided to try to group together the most beautiful non-Christian texts on the love of God.[24]

21 Weil, *Roots*, 107.
22 Weil, "Letter to Déodat Roché," *Weil Reader*, 83.
23 Ibid.
24 Father Perrin eventually published these texts under the title *Intuitions préchrétiennes* (Paris, 1951).

Such an idea—that the central inspirations of Christianity came from totally outside the Jewish and Roman traditions—was extremely radical. She became an extreme Hellenophile, to the chagrin of some of her friends (such as Father Perrin) who feared a drift into extremism and heresy. The point, however, is that Simone Weil's persistent religious focus in 1940-1942 was not unrelated to the terrible drama of Europe. In fact her studies seem to have been largely inspired by an effort to find a more helpful diagnosis to get to the bottom of the causes of Hitlerism. With this in mind, one understands her obsession with the Romans and her apocalyptic language in describing their influence in the West.

With time her researches led her to believe exactly the contrary about the historical background to the coming of Christ from that which most Christians are taught. She no longer saw God educating man, preparing him for divinity (as in certain Fathers of the Church, such as St. Irenaeus), through the achievements and perceptions of the Jews and the Romans. She thought, on the contrary, that Jesus had come to precisely those people, at that time in history, who needed him most.[25] If Christ had been born elsewhere, at a different time, everything would have been different: "If Christ had been born in India, He would have been worshipped as a God."[26]

The Roman Tradition in Western History

Simone Weil wrote most about the Romans when she was in London during the war, composing memoranda to influence the policies which the Free French were to follow after the Liberation. She was writing for tough, hard-minded men not particularly attuned to theological argumentation. Therefore her lines of analysis led to secular judgments relying on historical persuasion rather than assuming believing hearers moved by juggling articles of faith. The Romans, for her, need only be seen as a remarkably "rootless" people, similar to other imperialistic peoples also made cruel by their "uprootedness":

> Uprootedness is by far the most dangerous malady to which human societies are exposed, for it is a self-propagating one....
>   The Romans were a handful of fugitives who banded themselves together artificially to form a city, and deprived the Mediter-

25 There is the obvious precedent set by Jesus insisting that he be about among the sinners.
26 Her comment to Canon Vidal, reported in Pétrement, *Weil*, 2: 399.

ranean peoples of their individual manner of life, their country, traditions, past history to such an extent that posterity has taken them, at their own valuation, for the founders of civilization in these conquered territories. The Hebrews were escaped slaves and they either exterminated or reduced to servitude all the peoples of the Palestine.

Weil saw the Germans in the same light:

The Germans at the time Hitler assumed command over them were really—as he was never tired of repeating—a nation of proletarians, that is to say, uprooted individuals.... The Spaniards and Englishmen who, from the sixteenth century onward, massacred or enslaved coloured peoples, were adventurers almost without any contact with the fundamental life of their own respective countries.... Whoever is uprooted himself uproots others. Whoever is rooted in himself doesn't uproot others.[27]

In her view, the tendency of the Romans to uproot others had fateful results on their neighbours:

Rome, like every colonizing country, morally and spiritually uprooted the conquered countries. Such is always the effect of a colonial conquest. It was not a question of giving them back their roots. It was necessary they should be still further uprooted.[28]

One of the most effective tools with which the Romans uprooted peoples was their notion of patriotism, which—as we have seen—had a fateful influence on the West up through the age of Hitlerism. The modern notion of patriotism, she argued, flowed straight from it:

The Romans really were an atheistic and idolatrous people; not idolatrous with regard to images made of stone and bronze, but idolatrous with regard to themselves. It is this idolatry of self which they have bequeathed to us in the form of patriotism.[29]

And this idolatrous form of patriotism promoted a brutal attitude toward conquered peoples, deracinating and humiliating them rather than merely subduing them.

Weil saw an example of Roman cultural imperialism in the conquest of Gaul:

The Romans, so it is said, civilized Gaul. There was no art there before Gallo-Roman art; no thought before the Gauls had the

27 Weil, *Roots*, 47-48.
28 Weil, "Letter to a Priest," in *Gateway*, 146.
29 Weil, *Roots*, 141.

privilege of reading the philosophical productions of Cicero; and so on.

We know, as it were, nothing about Gaul; but the scanty indications we do possess are sufficient to prove all that to be a lie:

... We have it from Caesar that the course of study pursued by the Druids lasted twenty years, and consisted in learning by heart poems about the divine nature and the universe. . . .

Thus this people possessed a whole ocean of sacred poetry whose inspiration we are only able to form some idea of through the works of Plato.

All that disappeared when the Romans wiped out the entire collection of Druids for being guilty of the crime of patriotism.[30]

Having destroyed an ancient heritage, what did the Romans introduce into Gaul? They introduced the cruelty of the "rootless" Romans:

The Romans ... instituted in Gaul and everywhere else the putting to death of thousands of innocent people, not in order to do honour to the gods, but in order to amuse the crowds. That was their institution *par excellence*, one they set up wherever they went; and yet we dare regard them as civilizers.[31]

T. S. Eliot, otherwise a great admirer of Simone Weil, could not go along with her picture of the Roman conquest of Gaul. He thought it reflected an intellectual vice to which she was sometimes given:

In one quarter she sees only what she can admire; in another, she repudiates without discrimination. Because she dislikes the Roman Empire she dislikes Virgil. Her admirations, when not motivated by her dislikes, seem at least intensified by them. . . . when, in order to enhance her denunciation of the Romans, she attempts to make out a case for the culture of the Druids, we do not feel that our meagre knowledge of that vanished society gives any ground for her conjectures.[32]

Most scholars would doubtless see some truth in Eliot's objection to Weil's lavish praise of Druidic culture, and such wholesale admiration does seem a bit forced. Eliot notes elsewhere a contrast between Weil's almost superhuman "humility" and what seemed "an almost outrageous arrogance"; and he noted that, since she was only thirty-three, one could not judge her philosophical generalizations in the

30 Ibid., 222.
31 Ibid., 223.
32 T. S. Eliot, "Préface," in *Roots*, x.

same way as someone twenty or thirty years older. On the other hand, Eliot cautioned that he did not know how good a Greek scholar she was, how well-read she became in the civilizations of the Eastern Mediterranean, or if she could read the Upanishads in Sanskrit and if she really appreciated the difficulties of that very highly developed language.[33] One should recall here that Eliot admired certain "Roman" features in the Christian Church and Weil's severe criticism of this tradition ran counter to important elements of his own religious outlook. Still, for all his reservations, Eliot did not hesitate to call Weil "a woman of genius"[34] despite the fact that many of her historical generalizations contradicted prominent themes in his own essays on *Christianity and Culture*.[35]

Even if we find some of Weil's historical theses exaggerated—and we might wonder if there was not a certain arrogance in her trumpeting such broad historical generalizations at so young an age—there is nevertheless an undoubted brilliance and striking originality to many of her comments on history. It seems they were coloured by her lived experience—factory work, illness, war—more than by years of mere reflection in the reading room of the *Bibliothèque Nationale*. Eliot wondered if the apparent "egotism" of Simone Weil was not in fact a profound selflessness, and if the exaggerations of her polemics did not come from the fact that ". . . all her thought was so intensely lived, that the abandonment of any opinion required modifications in her whole being—a process which could not take place painlessly, or in the course of a conversation." And if one examines some of her exaggerations—such as her insistence on the value and complexity of Druidic culture—one finds many of them supportable (e.g., her defense of Druidic civilization would seem to find substantiation, not only in the discipline of Anthropology since Levi-Strauss, but also in the more recent interest in "ethnicity").

Simone Weil never intended to be an academic historian and several of her historical theses can be challenged.[36] Nevertheless, like Nietzsche, she must be adjudged an original and creative thinker about history.

33 Ibid., vi, ix.
34 Ibid., vi.
35 Cf. T. S. Eliot, "The Idea of a Christian Society" and "Notes Toward the Definition of Culture," in his *Christianity and Culture* (New York, 1949).
36 E.g., Professor Simone Fraisse, an admirer of Simone Weil, charges that her "eulogy" of the Cathars was inspired by the *Chanson de la Croisade contre les Albigeois*, "a literary work based on uncertain documentation" (Simone Fraisse, *Simone Weil, Philosophe, historienne et mystique*, edited by Gilbert Kahn [Paris, 1978], 165).

De-Romanizing Christianity

Simone Weil's attack on Rome was one which, on the surface, most historians and political scientists could easily weigh in the light of history. But her argument was far more complex and difficult to assess than at first glance. It was initially bound up in her very distinctive notion of the evolution of religion in the West. Like Nietzsche, again, she saw change in religious perceptions, in the sense of God, as absolutely vital in the historical transformation of Europe. Like Nietzsche too, she discerned a process whereby the original Christian Gospels were "Romanized" to create the distinctive religiosity of Western culture. In direct contradiction to Nietzsche, however, she saw this "Romanization" process as terrible and tragic.[37]

For Weil, the Romans succeeded in imposing on Christians a sense of time, of the historical process, of God's relationship with men which was not only non-Christian but utterly false. This was not merely a religious matter but a subject of great importance to all of the Western experience, for Roman religiosity entailed practical and down to earth attitudes of great importance. Notable here was the Roman distortion of the Christian doctrine of the Redemption. The Romans were said by her to have habitually abolished the ascetic and otherworldly spiritualities of subject cultures, and thus the melding of their insights with those of the Christians. Instead the Romans substituted "an historical conception concerning the Redemption, making of the latter a temporal operation instead of an eternal one." She saw this notion, in turn, fostering the modern idea of progress. Progress was but a laicized version of the Roman idea of redemption, and it had become "the bane of our times."

One of the great faults of the belief in progress for Simone Weil was that it made morality so relative: epic deeds in the fourteenth century were seen as great and good things in their time, but "primitive" by our own modern period.[38] Thus, she argued, the dogma of progress brought "dishonour on goodness by turning it into a question of fashion":[39]

> It is, moreover, solely because the historical mind consists in accepting the word of murderers unquestioningly that this dogma

37 Though Nietzsche did once observe that "the good news was followed by the very worst: St. Paul." While Nietzsche's attitude toward "Rome versus Christianity" was clear, his view of Jesus himself was (as Walter Kaufmann observes) ambiguous.
38 Weil, Roots, 229-30.
39 Cf. Nietzsche: "There are no moral phenomena; just moral interpretations of phenomena."

seems to correspond so admirably to the facts. When from time to
time a shaft of horror manages to pierce the opaque sensibility of a
reader of Livy, he says to himself, "those were the customs of the
time."[40]

For her, goodness and cruelty were perennial qualities and tied up
with the very essence of Christ's revelation. The notion of progress
undermined men's notions of what was good and bad by assuming
that Christ's Redemption was a mere event in time—merely of this
world.

For a Christian familiar with Western history, she thought, the
very notion of progress was totally unacceptable. The Christian had to
evaluate man's pilgrimage on earth in view of the love of God and
progress there was a subject to question. Simone Weil raised this
issue and came to the contrary conclusion—one quite humbling for
Jews and Christians who could accept it:

> Before the advent of Christianity, an indeterminate number of men,
> both in Israel and outside it, may *possibly* have gone as far as the
> Christian saints in the love and in the knowledge of God.
>   ... it is doubtful whether since Christ's time there has been
> more love and knowledge of God in Christendom than in certain
> non-Christian countries, such as India.[41]

For Westerners who simply assumed the moral and spiritual
superiority of their own culture, such a generalization would be a
dash of cold water. If "Christian civilization" had not been able to
demonstrate more love and knowledge of God than other peoples,
what does this tell us about the validity and worth of Christ's redemptive activities? Here Weil offered a paradoxical observation worthy of
Pascal: "The proof that the content of Christianity existed before
Christ is that since his day there have been no very noticeable changes
in men's behaviour."[42]

This of course was a terrible contradiction: the religion founded
by the Son of God himself, which profited from his presence and
special revelations, seemed to have made little "progress" in inspir-
ing men with greater love or knowledge of God. How was this possible? Again, a return to Weil's whole philosophy of history is necessary. Why had Christ not been born in India where "he would have
been worshipped as a God?" What were the roles of the Jews and

40 Weil, *Roots*, 230.
41 Weil, "Letter to a Priest," in *Gateway*, 134.
42 Ibid., 108.

Romans in Christ's redemptive activity, and in subsequent human history? And Nazism?

Tied together with Simone Weil's idea of the almost unprecedented brutality of Roman patriotism was their distinctive style in the practice of slavery. For her slavery not only had, as we have seen, a decisive influence on the political heritage of the West but also on the religious sensibility of Westerners as well. One's perception of God's relationship with the world, his Providence, was all important:

> Faith in Providence consists in being certain that the universe in its totality is in conformity to the will of God . . . that is to say, that in this universe good outweighs evil. . . . Thus the object of this certitude is an eternal and universal dispensation constituting the foundation of an invariable order in the world. Divine Providence is never represented in any other form, unless I am mistaken, either in the sacred texts of the Chinese, the Indians, and the Greeks, or in the Gospels.

This quasi-universal religious insight, she argued, was radically altered by the Romans in their own peculiar adoption of Christianity, with fateful consequences: ". . . when the Christian religion was officially adopted by the Roman Empire, the impersonal aspect of God and of Divine Providence was thrust into the background. God was turned into a counterpart of the Emperor."[43] Earlier we saw how Weil thought that the notions of patriotism of the Romans and the Jews were parallel: they were both brutal and idolatrous, both justified the oppression of the weak by the strong. Related to this similarity of attitudes was a common theme in the two peoples' religiosity. Both the Jews and the Romans, whatever their differences in other areas, had a common notion of slavery, central to both their cosmologies. As for the Jews:

> In the texts dating from before the exile, Jehovah's juridical relationship to the Hebrews is that of master to his slaves. They had been Pharaoh's slaves; Jehovah, having taken them out of Pharaoh's hands, has succeeded to Pharaoh's rights. . . . He orders them indifferently to do good or evil, but far more often evil, and in either case they have to obey. It matters little that they should be made to obey from the basest motives, provided that orders are duly executed.

As for the Romans, "Such a conception as this was exactly on a par with the feelings and intelligence of the Romans. With them slavery had undermined and degraded all human relations."[44] Thus, Simone

43 Weil, *Roots*, 271.
44 Ibid.

Weil argued, besides the remarkable political affinity between the Jews and the Romans, there was an unusual spiritual affinity as well. The Father of the Gospels which the Christians worshipped would seem to have little to do with the Emperor or Jehovah slave-master God, but Simone Weil maintained that Christianity "owing to its historical origin, has been unable to purge itself" of its Judaic element. Thus Christianity was not only unable to prevent this unholy fusion of perverse senses of God, it was fatefully corrupted by it, right from the beginning.

What, one must ask, was the Roman stake in all of this? Why did the Romans adopt Christianity after all? Here her interpretation was cynical; she was able to draw another one of her parallels between the Romans and the Hitlerites. She thought, first of all, that the Romans were not sincerely attracted to Christianity. They were pure atheists and pure materialists who feared the spirituality of their neighbours:

> The Romans could not tolerate anything rich in spiritual content. Love of God is a dangerous fire whose contact could prove fatal to their wretched deification of slavery. So they ruthlessly destroyed spiritual life under all its forms. . . . They wiped out the Druids in Gaul; destroyed the Egyptian religious cults; drowned in blood and brought into disrepute by ingenious calumnies the worship of Dionysus. We know what they did to Christians at the beginning.

Thus the Romans had a broad contempt for spiritual values. But history demonstrates, Weil continued, that pure atheists and pure materialists—however thoroughgoing—are seldom entirely comfortable with this position among their fellow human beings. The Romans were no exception:

> . . . They felt ill at ease in their all too vulgar idolatry. Like Hitler they knew the value of a deceptive exterior of spirituality. They would have liked to take the outer coverings of an authentic religious tradition to act as a cloak for their all too visible atheism. Hitler, too, would be pleased enough to found a religion.[45]

Thus the Roman interest in Christianity was, at best, feigned, at worst, coldly rapacious. The Romans, like the Nazis, needed Christianity only as a useful camouflage. But how could the Christians cooperate with such an anomalous usurpation? Here, she argued, the Christians succumbed in the face of Roman brutality and their own disappointed hopes:

45   Ibid., 276.

The Christians consented when they were too worn out with being massacred, too disheartened at not seeing the arrival of the triumphant end of the world. It is thus that the Father of Christ, accommodated to the Roman fashion, became a master and owner of slaves. Jehovah furnished the necessary means of transition. There was no longer the least difficulty about welcoming him. There was no longer any dispute over property between the Roman emperor and him, since the destruction of Jerusalem.[46]

For Simone Weil this transfiguration of the Father of Christ into a master and owner of slaves was a cultural event with enormous implications, felt well into the twentieth century. While Nietzsche saw "Chanadala values," world-hating, poisonous attitudes, corrupting Western man when the early Christians (or the socialists) succeeded in seducing others with their ideas, Simone Weil saw the Romans poisoning Christianity with their brutally earthbound attitude toward religion: "... Roman idolatry has defiled everything—... it is the mode of worship. ... If a Christian worships God with a heart disposed like that of a pagan of Rome in the homage rendered to the Emperor, that Christian is an idolator also."[47]

Simone Weil's judgment as to the extent of this defilement of Christianity by the Roman sense of God left a bleak picture. It was not a mere error by the ignorant and superstitious masses from which the Christian intellectual and spiritual elite were exempt. In fact one of the most prominent examples of a mind exhibiting the Roman conception of God which she cited was the most prominent French Catholic thinker of her generation: Jacques Maritain—and she provided texts from his writings to illustrate her point.[48] The Roman disease affected all levels and sections of the Church.

What could be done about recapturing the true spirit of Christianity? How could one go about de-Romanizing oneself, or de-Romanizing the Church? Here Weil laid great stress on the importance of mystics and mysticism. Mysticism, she thought, had preserved the truly Christian inspiration. If one studied the mystical tradition of the Catholic Church, one could uncover "another" faith precisely like that which she advocated:

46 Ibid., 277.
47 Ibid.
48 Ibid., 277-78. Maritain wrote influential books on Christian political philosophy in those years, notably *Freedom in the Modern World* (London, 1936); *Integral Humanism*, rev. ed. (New York, 1968); *Scholasticism and Politics* (New York, 1940); and *France, My Country, through the Disaster* (New York and Toronto, 1941).

> In the mystic traditions of the Catholic Church, one of the main objects of the purifications through which the soul has to pass is the total abolition of the Roman conception of God. So long as a trace of it remains, union through love is impossible.[49]

Simone Weil was compelled by a prophet's anguish over the corruption of Christianity to place her hope for Christianity in mysticism and mystics. And the tragedy of the Catholic Church, for her, was the historic strangulation of the mystics' impulse. This suppression, in turn, came not from a concern for orthodoxy but from worldly greed and ambition:

> ... The spiritual influence of the Mystics was powerless to destroy this conception in the Church as it was destroyed in their own hearts, because the Church needed it as the Empire before had needed it. It was necessary for the Church's temporal dominion.

And this persistent defeat of the mystics explained the persistent corruption of the Church: "... the Roman spirit of imperialism and domination has never loosened its hold over the Church sufficiently for the latter to be able to abolish the Roman conception of God."[50]

If the history of the West has been the long story of the recurrent defeat of the mystics, is there any hope for purifying Christianity? Was the "Romanized" Christianity part of the human condition? Was it possible for the masses, not only the mystics, to embrace Christianity but leave behind Roman barbarisms? Given Weil's strong hostility to the notion of progress it is evident that she did not, like her contemporary Teilhard de Chardin, foresee an inevitable "Christification," or necessary future triumph of a truly Christian value system. In fact her view of history is in many ways completely antithetical to that of the Jesuit paleontologist and theologian of evolution, despite their common devotion to the person of Christ. For Teilhard there was a necessary progress in love at the very heart of the universe. He thought, in particular, that there was, from generation to generation, a qualitative increase in the love experienced within married couples. This was one key to the inevitable world-wide recognition of the value and justice of Christ's teachings on Charity.[51] Teilhard, incredible as it may seem in retrospect, still foresaw the clash of forces in Europe in the late 1930s and early 1940s as part of the process of the spiritualization of mankind.[52] For Simone Weil, in contrast, the Nazis gave the lie

49 Ibid., 278.
50 Ibid., 278-79.
51 Cf. P. Teilhard de Chardin, The Divine Milieu (New York, 1960).
52 The Phenomenon of Man (New York, 1959), his best-known work, was based upon

to all optimistic notions of inevitable progress and theories about qualitative advances in human relationships. The cruelty and brutality of the Nazis, she argued, was qualitatively the same as that of the Romans: "The writings of the Greek historians leave one . . . with the clearest impression that the brutality of the Romans horrified and paralyzed their contemporaries in exactly the same way as that of the Germans today."[53] If the evil of the Romans, her obsession, was equalled by that of the Nazis in the twentieth century, how could one advance any theories about qualitative advances in human relationships? That the level of moral evil remained relatively constant in the world was evident from the situation in France in 1943. Her country, she thought, was subject to a brutal domination in precisely the same way as the Greeks had suffered under the Romans. And she imagined that "children in the Greek towns used openly to pelt collaborators with stones and call them traitors, with the same indignation we feel today."[54] In a Europe of Nazis, Vichy, and collaboration, how could one seriously speak of a progressive tendency toward freedom, spirituality, or more humane personal relationships? The Nazis refuted all linear interpretations of history. We have already seen how Simone Weil refused to grant any progress in knowledge or love of God in the West—or even any progress in goodness since the time of Christ.

Weil's metaphor about history—that "drops of purity" sparkle at odd intervals in its tissue of harsh and cruel events—is a good capsule summary of her doubts about incarnating truly Christian values in a generalized way in any particular period or culture. Nevertheless "drops of purity" do sparkle in history for her, and it is interesting to consider her examples of them to get an idea of where her philosophy of history might have gone had she lived long enough to develop it.

The Cathars and Romantic Love

Simone Weil's interest in the Cathars and the whole civilization of Languedoc was stimulated by her good friend Simone Pétrement, a former student of Alain, who pursued a serious scholarly interest in neo-platonic philosophy. We noted how Weil had thought that the Cathars, almost alone in the West, had remained faithful to the original Christian inspiration. From that assumption

a profound belief in evolutionary progress and was composed in the late 1930s. His published correspondence during these years also reflects this perception of events.
53 Weil, *Roots*, 230.
54 Ibid., 104.

she sketched out her own view of the turning points in Western civilization, and pictured the defeat of the authentic Christian tradition as avertible and rather tragic:

> The so-called barbarians, of whom many, doubtless, originally came from Thrace and had imbibed the spiritual influence of the Mysteries, took Christianity seriously; with the result that we very nearly had a Christian civilization. We can discern the dawn of it in the eleventh and twelfth centuries. The countries to the south of the Loire, which formed the principal radiating centre for it, were impregnated at the same time both with Christian spirituality and ancient spirituality; at any rate, it is true that the Albigenses were Manicheans, and consequently inspired not only by Persian thought, but also by Gnostic, Stoic, Pythagorean, and Egyptian thought. The civilization, which was then in embryo, would have been free from all taint of slavery, the different trades would have occupied the place of honour.[55]

Thus Weil thought that the best traditions of antiquity did in fact survive for a limited time and place in Europe even after the defilement of Christianity by the Roman and Hebraic traditions. And this was not exclusively confined to the Cathar sect in odd moments but rather extended to an entire region of Europe, and for a period of centuries. She only sketched out its principal characteristics and saw suggestions of it in various past political, social, and artistic flowerings: in what seemed to be a sort of "syndicalist democracy" described by Machiavelli in the Florence of the twelfth century; the way in which both knights and workmen united to defend Toulouse against the crusade of Simon de Montfort; the religiously inspired corporations of the Middle Ages; and also in cultural achievement:

> All we need to do is look at a Romanesque Church, listen to a Gregorian melody, read one of the perfect poems of the troubadors, or better still, the liturgical texts, in order to recognize that art and religious faith were indistinguishable from one another as they were in ancient Greece at its highest point.[56]

For her this possibility of a Christian civilization was destroyed by the imperialistic scourge of Romanism. One well known example of the spirit of Romanist aggression which she cited was Saint Bernard's struggle against Abelard. Again, it was not just the Albigensian sect which was suppressed but the possibility of a different direction in

55   Ibid., 297-98.
56   Ibid., 298.

Western civilization. At the beginning of the thirteenth century, she thought, this civilization was still in the process of formation but it was destroyed with the ruin of its principal centre—the lands south of the Loire—and with the establishment of the Inquisition and stifling of religious thought in the name of orthodoxy by men like St. Bernard. The Romanist impulse, she argued, upset the sort of equilibrium between religious dogma and freedom of thought, and this perverted subsequent Western development and led to a period of cultural decline:

> The conception of orthodoxy, by rigorously separating the domain relating to the welfare of souls, which is that of an unconditional subjection of the mind to external authority, from the domain relating to so-called profane matters, in which the intelligence remains free, makes impossible that mutual penetration of the religious and the profane, which would be the essence of a Christian civilization.... The thirteenth and fourteenth centuries and the early part of the fifteenth are the period of medieval decadence. They show the progressive degradation and final eclipse of a civilization which was stillborn, the progressive desiccation of a single germ cell.[57]

Interestingly enough, this idea that there was a distinctive culture in the South of France which produced the troubadors, Provençal poetry, and Catharism, and made a contribution of great importance to Western development was also shared by another Christian intellectual who travelled in the same circles as Simone Weil, but drew different conclusions about the significance of these phenomena. For Denis de Rougemont in his classic study *Love in the Western World*[58] most of the very forces which Weil saw as producing the West's best hope for a Christian culture had in fact originated the cult of romantic passionate love in the West—a cult whose evolution he traced from troubador love ballads, through Romeo and Juliet, to Rousseau's *Nouvelle Héloise*, and culminating in Wagner's *Tristan and Isolde*. For de Rougemont, a "Barthian" Protestant, the modern obsession with romantic love, which he found totally incompatible with the values represented by a Christian conception of marriage, had its origins in this tradition. He found the distinctive culture which originated in southern France to have been an aberrant phenomenon from a Christian point of view—one which had an important influence in profaning sexual relationships in the West.[59]

---

57 Ibid., 298-99.
58 Denis de Rougemont, *Love in the Western World* (New York, 1966).
59 See ibid., 78-86.

How could two prominent Christian thinkers of the same generation, who agreed that the same well-defined culture was of great
historical significance, differ so profoundly on the compatibility of
this culture with Christian values? How could Simone Weil, often
considered an extreme ascetic, be linked to the origin of modern
tendencies toward eroticism and the glorification of sexuality? And
how could de Rougemont find the same civilization which Weil found
so truly Christian in inspiration, to be so essentially anti-Christian?
Here it is important to note that, while both de Rougemont and Weil
agreed that one of the most important sources of the Albigensian
culture was Manichaeism, they totally differed in their evaluation of
that particular tendency. For de Rougemont it was a pernicious heresy
which over the centuries did Christianity an enormous amount of
harm. For Simone Weil, on the contrary, the Manichees had contributed to, and helped preserve, the authentic Christian spirit: "There is
not, as far as I can see, any real difference—save in forms of
expression—between Manichean and Christian conceptions concerning the relationship between good and evil."[60] Simone Weil did not
see anything fundamentally incompatible between a religion which
perceived evil as rooted in the flesh and matter and the Christian view
of the world.[61]

It is at this point that de Rougemont and Weil diverge over the
import of the Manichean tradition. For de Rougemont the Manichean
aversion to matter and the human body fostered the distinctive attitudes toward love which the troubadors expressed in their poetry
and the Cathars in their religious culture. At the conclusion of his
analysis de Rougemont presented a paradox: the Cathars and
troubadors, who invented and diffused the doctrine of passionate
romantic love, were in fact compelled to celebrate romantic love
because of their distaste for sexual intercourse. The Christian conception of sex, according to him, frankly accepted the connection between love, sexual intercourse, and the procreation of children; the
Manichean did not. And the Manichean tradition—via the troubadors, Cathars, et al.—was, despite appearances, behind modern
eroticism and the doctrine of sexual self-fulfillment which was leading to divorce on a massive scale and a whole host of other affronts to
Christian morality. Reading between the lines, de Rougemont (quite a
Romanist for all of his Swiss Protestantism) would have found the
persecution of the troubadors, and the crusade against the Albigen-

---

60 Weil, "Letter to a Priest," in *Gateway*, 121.
61 In a letter to Déodat Roché, which has only come to light recently, she went even
    further in her expression of admiration for Manicheans.

sians, at least partially justifiable. Their distortions introduced vices and errors with enormous implications, which disrupted families and adversely affected millions of human beings.[62]

Simone Weil, on the other hand, saw the persecution of devout religious people like the Cathars—who preached a doctrine of love and desired only to be good according to their own lights—quite differently:

> ... The perfect ones among the Cathars ... were in relation to a host of theologians what the Good Samaritan of the parable is in relation to the priest and Levite. In that case, what are we to think of those who allowed them to be massacred and gave their blessing to Simon de Montfort?
>
> The Church ought to have learned from this parable never to excommunicate anyone who practices the love of his neighbour.[63]

De Rougemont drew much sharper distinction between "love" and "lust" than did Simone Weil, and he found much of the "love" celebrated by the Manichean tradition damnable from the Christian point of view. He thought the revived Manichaeism of the Cathars produced a profound contempt for the body and sexual intercourse which radically distinguished between the soul and the physical flesh. This inspired the ballads of the troubadors to a secret contempt for sexual intercourse which led to it being taken "less seriously"— hence to an abandonment of Christian sexual standards relating to it. Thus "love of neighbour" took a form among the Manicheans, according to de Rougemont, which the church could scarcely endorse.[64]

It is true that part of Simone Weil's interest in the Cathars came from their unusual conception of the relationship between soul and body. But this was in the context of her entire intellectual effort, and all part of her general juxtaposition of Christian tradition against the teaching of Jesus. On this issue her approach was as innovative as in many others, and became ever more so as she proceeded in her study of Christian scriptures. For example, in one of her later meditations on the doctrine of the resurrection of the flesh she wandered far outside accepted Christian orthodoxy:

> The living flesh which must perish, and the "spiritual flesh" (*pneumatikê*—should we keep in mind the Phythagorean theory of the *pneuma* contained in the semen?) which is eternal. The rela-

---

62 De Rougemont, *Love*, 289-338.
63 Weil, "Letter to a Priest," in *Gateway*, 121.
64 Cf. de Rougemont, *Love*, 85-86.

tionship between this doctrine and the importance attached to chastity. . . .

The study of Hindu doctrines casts a much more vivid light thereon than any Christian text that I know of. Christians have never said, as far as I am aware, *why* chastity (and more especially virginity) possess a spiritual value. This is a serious lacuna, and one that keeps a great many souls from Christ.[65]

Thus Simone Weil could not share Denis de Rougemont's strong condemnation of the culture of romantic passionate love vis-à-vis Christian attitudes toward the body. As far as she was concerned, this was another area in which Christian traditions needed serious critical examination to see if they conformed to the teachings of Christ. She certainly considered it possible, perhaps even likely, that the Cathars—since their sense of charity was so impressive—might well have come closer to a correct view of the body than the supposed Christian "tradition." Some of her comments on love certainly put her outside of the mainstream with regard to sexuality at the time she was writing. For example, she wrote "In Plato's eyes carnal love is a degraded image of true love. Chaste human love (conjugal fidelity) is a less degraded image of it. Only in the stupidity of the present day could the idea of sublimation arise."[66] Or again: "To love purely is to consent to distance, it is to adore the distance between ourselves and that which we love."[67]

Simone Weil's ideas on love were necessarily closely tied to her radical critique of contemporary Christianity in the light of Christ's sayings. Nazism represented the spiritual bankruptcy of a civilization proudly calling itself "Christian" and led Weil to speculation about if and when that civilization had indeed ever been Christian. Thus her view of history focussed instead on those "drops of purity" of Christians living in a truly Christian way which the West produced.

Although the Cathars did play an important role in Weil's view of history, it would be an error not to qualify her admiration for them. In the first place her defense of them (as so many of her other more shocking "defensive" positions) was meant to serve as a corrective to hasty dismissals of their significance. And in the second place, she saw other times and other places in which men came close to incarnating a Christian civilization (for example, she cited the early Renaissance, which saw a certain revival of the spirit of the twelfth century, an admiration for classical Greece, Pythagoras, and Plato all in har-

65 Weil, "Letter to a Priest," in *Gateway*, 136-37.
66 Weil, "Criteria for Wisdom," in *Weil Reader*, 358.
67 Ibid., 360.

mony with the Christian faith—until it was rapidly succeeded by what she called the "second Renaissance" "with quite the opposite tendency"). A Christian civilization *was* a distinct possibility and this is why she stressed the importance of the Cathars. She liked to see them as Christian Platonists who were able to create a culture in which "the highest thought dwelt within a whole human environment and not only in the minds of certain individuals."[68] If such a civilization had existed once it might well be created again, and so, for her, the Cathars were a great sign of hope in history.

The hope represented by an attempt at Christian civilization was particularly important given the spiritual desert in the early 1940s:

> Not since the dawn of history, except for a certain period of the Roman Empire, has Christ been so absent as today. The separation of religion from the rest of social life, which seems natural even to the majority of Christians nowadays, would have been judged monstrous by antiquity.[69]

And what was so troubling about the massive despiritualization of an age which produced Stalin and Hitler was the responsibility of the Christian Church for this situation. This, too, strongly coloured her historical perspective because, rather than comfortably assuming the Church to be the persistent historical antithesis to atheism and totalitarianism, she dared to suggest the contrary—that the Church herself may have helped nurture these sinister anti-Christian forces: "After the fall of the Roman Empire, which had been totalitarian, it was the Church that was the first to establish a rough sort of totalitarianism in Europe in the thirteenth century after the war with the Albigenses. This tree bore much fruit."[70]

Thus it was the modern spiritual desert, the absence of religion from all aspects of life, that made Weil think back to periods such as the twelfth century, when Christ's teaching endured in small, beleaguered corners of Europe. She saw a great need to revive such a hope in a culture requiring "de-Romanization" which even the Christian Church did not seem to be able to provide. As she wrote to Déodat Roché:

> Never has a revival of this kind of thought been so necessary as today. We are living at a time when most people feel, confusedly but keenly, that what was called enlightenment in the 18th century,

---

68 "Letter to Déodat Roché," in *Weil Reader*, 84.
69 "The Love of God and Affliction," in ibid., 465.
70 "Spiritual Autobiography," in ibid., 25.

including the sciences, provides an insufficient spiritual diet; but this feeling is now leading humanity into the darkest paths. There is an urgent need to refer back to those great epochs which favoured the kind of spiritual life of which all that is most precious in science and art is no more than a somewhat imperfect reflection.[71]

Simone Weil's reflections on history, diffuse and incomplete as they may appear, demonstrate the unity and coherence of her thought. Like Nietzsche, her analysis of history was grounded on a perception of the implications of dramatic transformations in the evolving sense of God in the West. The factors which were important in this evolution were common to both Nietzsche and Weil. Their respective evaluations of the moral and spiritual results of these phenomena, however, differed profoundly. For her, one of the most pressing problems about the modern world was the corruption of Christianity. Once bound to her sharply defined outline of the figure of Christ, the greater part of her intellectual effort was devoted toward trying to understand the reasons, and find a remedy, for distortions of it. For her, religious distortions were not merely of peripheral concern; they were connected—sometimes indirectly, sometimes directly—with scourges such as Stalinism and Hitlerism. The prevalent sense of God in the West was the heart of the problem:

> Let us imagine some great Roman magnate owning vast estates and numbers of slaves, and then multiply this to bring it up to the dimensions of the universe itself. Such is the conception of God which, in fact, rules over a portion of Christianity, and which has perhaps more or less infected the whole of Christianity, with the exception of the Mystics.[72]

Much like an ancient Hebrew prophet—and atheistic moderns like Friedrich Nietzsche and Albert Camus—Simone Weil condemned the religious sensitivities of her contemporaries. But instead of proposing the eradication of Christianity, she held hopes for its ultimate purification.

In her determination to purify Western religiosity, Weil was singularly ungenerous to Jews and Christians alike. Jews were understandably dubious about her severity toward the spirit of ancient Israel at a time when (albeit unknown to her)[73] Jews were being exterminated. Several Catholics deplored her violent criticism of a Church suffering under the pressures of Hitlerism and fascism. One

---

71 "Letter to Déodat Roché," in ibid., 84-85.
72 Weil, *Roots*, 280.
73 Maurice Schumann, "Présentation de Simone Weil," in *Simone Weil*, 18.

might rejoin, however, that the acrimony of this criticism is due to the fact that, beyond sympathizing with the Jews and Catholics in their difficulties, Weil always insisted on their assessing their own responsibilities for the racist and totalitarian abominations of the day. If a prophet is without honour in his own country, this Catholic Jewess died understandably unacceptable to both of her traditions. She had the audacity to suggest that the Jewish, Roman, and Catholic traditions alike be charged with a critical eye for their own, less obvious, responsibility for Hitler. It was far easier and more comfortable to dismiss Hitler as a lunatic, satanic figure, or a "German," than to address issues that so offended, and still offend, a good number of Jews, "Romans," and Catholics.

Her friend Maurice Schumann, voice of the Free French, recalled a conversation in 1942. Though they had not yet learned of the extermination camps in Europe, Weil employed with "a marvellous and atrocious premonition," the word "holocaust." She was troubled by several sections of the Old Testament—notably on Saul and the Amelikites—which seemed to justify genocide: "How can we condemn a holocaust today," she wondered, "if we have not condemned all past holocausts?"[74]

74 Ibid.

College of the Rockies
Library

5
RELIGION

Possession by Christ

In her letter of Spring 1941 to Father Perrin (later published as her *Spiritual Autobiography*), Simone Weil described an evolution in her life which culminated in Christ's "taking possession" of her. She did not describe herself being thunderstruck, like Paul on the road to Damascus, by an unexpected religious experience. Rather, in retrospect, she ascribed a certain undramatic inevitability to the events at the heart of her intellectual and spiritual awakening:

> After my year in the factory, before going back to teaching, I had been taken by my parents to Portugal, and while there I left them to go alone to a little village. I was, as it were, in pieces, soul and body.... As I worked in the factory, undistinguishable to all eyes, including my own, from the anonymous mass, the affliction of others entered into my flesh and my soul.... There I received forever the mark of a slave, like the branding of the red-hot iron which the Romans put on the foreheads of their most despised slaves. Since then I have always regarded myself as a slave.
>
> In this state of mind then, and in a wretched condition physically, I entered the little Portuguese village which, alas was very wretched too.... It was the evening and there was a full moon. It was by the sea. The wives of the fishermen were going in procession to make a tour of the ships, carrying candles and singing what must certainly be very ancient hymns of a heart-rending sadness.... I have never heard anything so poignant.... There the conviction was suddenly borne in upon me that Christianity is pre-eminently

the religion of slaves, that slaves cannot help belonging to it, and I among the others.[1]

The consciousness of being a slave, of sharing the slaves' lot, came to Weil very early in her life—through her empathy for the poor and oppressed and her experiencing their conditions. What was new in her Portuguese experience was the realization that Christianity was the normal, inevitable, and true religion of the slave.[2] Previously she had thought revolutionary Marxism or *syndicalism* to be the true and proper religion of the oppressed. But her experiences of revolutionaries, her realization of their inadequacies and their shortcomings, made her see the "revolutionary" religion as that of the leaders, technicians, and rhetoricians of the oppressed; the slaves themselves were excluded. It was out of love for those whose afflictions had entered into her own "flesh and soul" that Simone Weil became Christian.

Assuming that one could only be properly "Christian" out of solidarity with slaves, Simone Weil characteristically focussed on the "essence" of this religion. This entailed full attention to Jesus himself. In 1937, visiting a twelfth century chapel in Assisi (which St. Francis used to frequent), she went on her knees in prayer for the first time. At Easter 1938, with an interest that was primarily aesthetic, Simone and her mother spent ten days at the Benedictine abbey of Solesmes, a centre for liturgical music. There, while again experiencing intense physical pain from the mysterious headaches which had begun to plague her, she gained a precious insight into the "slave religion," toward which she already felt so much solidarity:

> I was suffering from splitting headaches; each sound hurt me like a blow; by an extreme effort of concentration I was able to rise above this wretched flesh, . . . and to find a pure and perfect joy in the unimaginable beauty of the chanting and the words. This experience enabled me by analogy to get a better understanding of the possibility of loving divine love in the midst of affliction. . . . The thought of the Passion of Christ entered into my being once and for all.[3]

Having found her solidarity with the "religion of slaves," and nurturing the conviction that the essence of Jesus' passion was loving the love of God in the midst of suffering, she turned her attention to God

1 Weil, *Waiting for God*, 32-34.
2 Here again she not merely calls Nietzsche to mind but echoes him.
3 Ibid., 34.

himself. A fellow guest at the Abbey of Solesmes lent her a poem with a mystical focus, directed toward the love of God, and Simone Weil recited it again and again:

> I learned it by heart. Often, at the culminating point of a violent headache, I made myself say it over, concentrating all my attention upon it. . . . without my knowing it, the recitation had the virtue of a prayer. It was during one of these recitations that, as I told you, Christ Himself came down and took possession of me.[4]

This "possession" was doubtless less miraculous than it sounds. Simone Weil's religious thought is not amenable to direct divine interventions in human life, but rather clings to a profound sense of the lawfulness and order of the universe (what she called its "obedience of God"). Christ's "taking possession" of Simone Weil was less a supernatural event than the logical destination of the spiritual pilgrimage she had forced upon herself. She had pursued many courses in search of the truth and each one had become a blind alley. She had not sought out a religious or mystical experience. It seemed rather to be a sudden release at the end of a dull and twisting labyrinth—a light she had stumbled toward more by inevitability than choice:

> I had never read any mystical works because I had never felt any call to read them. . . . God in his mercy had prevented me from reading the mystics, so that it should be evident to me that I had not invented this absolutely unexpected contact.
> Yet I still half refused, not my love but my intelligence . . . one can never wrestle enough with God if one does so out of pure regard for the truth. Christ likes us to prefer truth to Him because, before being Christ, He is truth. If one turns aside from Him to go toward the truth, one will not go far before falling into His arms.[5]

Simone Weil's assertion that it was a determined concern for the truth that led, to her own surprise, to a concentration on the meaning of Christ fits in well with the lines of inquiry which she pursued since adolescence. Each route she followed toward an ultimate truth had proven insufficient. As a student she had embraced revolutionary Marxism only to find bitter disillusionment in confirmed horror stories from the Soviet Union. Her subsequent romance with non-Stalinist Marxism and frequenting of Trotskyist circles led to another kind of disillusionment. She crossed swords with Trotsky himself,

4 Ibid., 34-35.
5 Ibid., 36.

only to discover that the old Bolshevik leader was remarkably insensitive to the problem that seemed self-evidently primary to her: the oppressive working conditions of the proletariat. Her growing firsthand knowledge of the lives of factory and agricultural labourers had only widened her breach with the group at *La révolution prolétarienne*. Her subsequent flirtation with syndicalism, too, proved disillusioning when she found a similar lack of focus on workers among the elites of the trade union movement. Who, then, truly paid attention to workers? Charlot (Charlie Chaplin) and Jesus, the comic and the Christ.

There was, however, a problem even with Christ, in that a vast array of abuses had been committed in his name; nationalism, fascism, and even Nazism she could link with perverted forms of Christianity. She found she hated these subtle antecedents of fascism in the West with a profound and bitter hatred that her contemporaries found difficult to comprehend.

Her preoccupation with Jesus, coupled with a hatred of Stalinism and fascism, fueled Simone Weil's urgent turn to the activities and sayings of Jesus. "Jesus taught," she recalled, "a way of life, not a theology." And it was this way of life which Jesus taught that was—despite the impurities of the Christian churches—the ultimate antithesis to fascism, and the basic answer to the other most oppressive features of modern life. The sorry fate of the true Christian spirit through two thousand years was, she thought, the great drama and tragedy of Western history.

Non-Christians and the Love of God

Simone Weil did not simply "become a Christian" with all of the formal ceremony, personal drama, and social ramifications which this necessarily brought in her circle in her day. Several French Jewish intellectuals of her generation converted to Christianity—Jacques Ellul, Alexandre Marc, Raïssa Maritain, Maurice Schumann, to name a few. She knew several of them quite well (particularly Schumann, an old friend from the classes with Alain), but her "conversion" was to be different. In the first place she had been raised in such total ignorance of her Jewish heritage that neither she nor her brother even thought of themselves as being Jews when they were in their twenties.[6] Secondly, she never really "converted" to the Christian religion in the formal sense: she refused

6 Interview with André Weil in Weil, *Gateway*, 153.

Baptism and the sacraments éven on her deathbed![7] Thirdly, the sort of Christianity which she embraced was totally centred on the figure and teachings of Jesus—to the exclusion of the Old Testament and much Christian belief and tradition. Many Christians considered her "Christianity" eclectic, aberrant, and quite possibly heretical.

Immediately after her experience of Christ, she tells us in her "spiritual autobiography," Simone Weil had a whole series of realizations which allowed her to make sense of all her earlier, most important, experiences of truth in the ancient Greeks: Plato, she felt, was "a mystic" from the Christian point of view; the *Iliad* reflected all sorts of Christian truths; Dionysus and Osiris were "in a certain sense Christ Himself."[8] Of course it was not unprecedented for Christian converts to meld Christian and Greek insights, but Weil's boldness and originality in this exercise (e.g., her long commentary on the Iliad as reflecting Christian values), and the rapidity and ease with which she concluded that the two traditions were so remarkably harmonious was unusual. She even saw the Christian Gospels as in many ways the culmination of the distinctive Greek contribution to the human spirit:

> The Gospels are the last and most marvelous expression of Greek genius, as the *Iliad* is its first expression. The spirit of Greece made itself felt here not only by the fact of commanding us to seek to the exclusion of every other good "the kingdom of God and His righteousness" but also by its revelation of human misery, and by revealing that misery in the person of a divine being who is at the same time human. . . . The sense of human misery gives these accounts of the Passion that accent of simplicity which is the stamp of Greek genius.[9]

This perception of Christ as the embodiment of Greek wisdom and sensitivity characterized her view of history and her bitter hatred of the Roman influence on the Western tradition. It also encouraged that broad, new perspective with which she viewed the Christian religion. She could not fall upon Christian scriptures as if they held the one, exclusive revelation of the nature of God and his relationship with men. Rather she came to the Christian texts with the notion that they offered just one—albeit primary—set of insights into the nature of God. With her strong feelings about the wisdom and virtue of the

---

7 A recent story, perhaps apocryphal, has it that she was baptized a Catholic on her deathbed when she was too weak to resist and commented, "Well, all right, go ahead. I guess it can't do any harm."

8 Weil, "Spiritual Autobiography," in *Waiting for God*, 56.

9 Weil, "The *Iliad*, Poem of Might," in *Weil Reader*, 180.

Greeks and the perverseness of the Romans, she could not wholly embrace the writings of the Fathers of the Church, or even of Paul, with the same rapture with which she encountered the word of Christ. With the Hellenistic tradition being but one of the cultural forces which shaped Christianity, she was necessarily eclectic in her attitude toward that religion from the beginning.

In 1940 Simone Weil was attracted by several Hindu religious texts, as she explained to Father Perrin:

> In the spring of 1940 I read the Bhagavat-Gita. Strange to say it was in reading those marvelous words, words with such a Christian sound, put into the mouth of an incarnation of God, that I came to feel strongly that we owe an allegiance to religious truth which is quite different from the admiration we accord a beautiful poem, it is something far more categorical.[10]

If Simone Weil had an empathy that was capable of spanning the continents in its response to suffering, she also displayed a religious sensitivity that was capable of traversing oceans as well. The discovery of Christ, rather than locking her onto the Christian view of the world—like so many of her fellow converts—seemed rather to free her spirit for even wider horizons of spiritual experience.

Weil was drawn in the late 1930s to the ecumenical perspectives of the young intellectuals grouped around Emmanuel Mounier's review Esprit. The men and women of Esprit came from various religious traditions but were, like Simone Weil, generally of left-wing political instincts while convinced of the importance of spiritual values and commitments. Their conviction, often inspired by Péguy, was that the revolution would be spiritual or it could not be. At Esprit, there was the same sense of the insufficiencies of the traditional Left as her own. Esprit also had, in men like Jacques Ellul, the start of a thoroughgoing critique of the technological society. The Esprit group was united "in the spirit" despite various ideological divergences. Simone Weil came to accept and, in time, exceed even such a broad-minded position and was soon referring to "Krishna" where she might have said God or Christ. Soon she went beyond even Mounier's avant-garde review.[11]

From November 1941 to May 1942 Weil, who was studying Greek philosophy in collaboration with Father Perrin, wrote a series of essays relating to the religious sense displayed in the texts she had studied. It had been her intention to assemble a book of the most beautiful

10 Weil, "Spiritual Autobiography," in Waiting for God, 36.
11 On Simone Weil's relationship with Esprit see Hellman, Emmanuel Mounier.

non-Christian texts on the love of God.[12] Her concurrent reading of St. John of the Cross and the *Bhagavat-Gita* helped to convince her that there were no essential differences between the great mystics of the different religious traditions. And this realization in turn reinforced her reservations about the religious exclusiveness of the ancient Hebrews and was behind her comment to Canon Vidal that Jesus would have been treated very differently had He been born in India.[13]

Such empathy for non-Western religions reinforced Simone Weil's tendency to separate the New Testament from the "racist" Old Testament. Thus, before leaving occupied France for New York, she went to see Dom Clement and formulated her basic disagreements with Roman Catholic Orthodoxy. Here he gravely noted her sympathy for the heresies of Marcion (rooted in an implacable Old versus New Testament conflict), her notion that there may have been several pre-Christian incarnations of the Word (e.g., Krishna), her repugnance to believe that the "God" of Israel could have ordered the extermination of other peoples, and her reluctance to believe that the true knowledge of God was now more widely spread in modern Christian cultures than in antiquity or in India. The good monk sadly concluded that Simone Weil was an incorrigible heretic.[14]

Nurses against the S.S.

"Mais . . . elle est folle!" General de Gaulle is said to have remarked in London during the war on reading Simone Weil's project of resistance against Nazism, of her plan of creating a corps of heroic front-line nurses as an allied response to the spectacular but brutal courage of the S.S. While generals may have found it hopelessly naive, in the context of Simone Weil's intellectual and spiritual evolution the project made a great deal of sense, inspired as it was by what she considered to be the best of Western values, as well as those of the East, which could stand up to those of the Hitlerites.

Hitler's special troops, such as the S.S. or paratroopers, who demonstrated that they were not only ready to risk their lives for their cause but prepared to die for it were, Simone Weil argued, one of his most effective instruments. They were inspired, she thought, by a religion-substitute, an idolatry, which provoked a heroism which originated in extreme brutality. Thus the S.S. and similar corps were

---

12   These essays were later published by Father Perrin as the book *Intuitions préchrétiennes.*

13   Pétrement, *Weil*, 2: 399.

14   Ibid., 402.

inspired by a form of Hitlerism which corresponded perfectly to the spirit of the Nazi regime. They conformed to the designs of Hitler in their ability to strike everybody's imagination—driving their own people incessantly forward, provoking psychological disarray in their enemies, astonishing and impressing observers. Since the allies fought in a different spirit and with different motives, she thought, they should not respond to the S.S. by transforming their own youth into brutal fanatics like Hitler's, but rather find for them "a corresponding inspiration, but authentic and pure."

Weil proposed to start with a small nucleus of ten (or even fewer young women to form a special, very mobile body of front-line nurses which would always be at the point of greatest danger to give first-aid during battles. An elementary knowledge of nursing would suffice as nothing could be done under fire except dressing tourniquets and perhaps injections. What these women would require was a great deal of courage as they would, like the S.S., have to be prepared to offer their lives as a sacrifice. They would have to face as much, if not more, danger than the soldiers who are facing the most, "and this without being sustained by the offensive spirit, but, on the contrary, devoting themselves to the wounded and dying."[15]

These young women, Weil maintained, would be a perfect response to the S.S. and their Hitlerite fanaticism. Over against the Nazis' elite troops:

> ... we cannot claim to have more courage, because it would be quantitatively impossible. But we can and ought to demonstrate that our courage is qualitatively different, is courage of a more difficult and rarer kind. Theirs is a debased and brutal courage; it springs from the will to power and destruction. ...
> There could be no better symbol of our inspiration than the corps of women suggested here. ... a signal defiance of the inhumanity which the enemy has chosen for himself and which he compels us also to practice. ... A courage not inflamed by the impulse to kill but capable of supporting, at the point of greatest danger, the prolonged spectacle of wounds and agony, is certainly a rarer quality than that of the young S.S. fanatics. ... To transform our soldiers into brutal young fanatics like Hitler's youth is neither possible nor desirable. But their fire can be kindled to the full by keeping as clearly alive as possible the thought of the homes they are defending.[16]

15 Weil, "Plan for an Organization of Front-line Nurses," in Weil Reader, 96-98.
16 Ibid., 101-103.

The brave *Ubermensch* of the S.S. with their remarkable warrior qualities were often seen as a supreme embodiment of Nietzschean values. Now the front-line nurses were to be a perfect representative of those of Simone Weil. Nietzsche had seen Christian values as necessarily cowardly and worthy of contempt in any company of fighting men.[17] Simone Weil's nurses' corps was a perfect and direct response to this charge as well as to the entire fascist value system. Her nurses embodied that kind of true patriotism, rooted in compassion for one's country, which she had so effectively juxtaposed to the idolatrous nationalism and racism which she saw as the root inspiration of fascism. This form of patriotism, she argued, was not only capable of summoning forth a bravery as impressive as that of the S.S., but one totally devoid of hatred or cruelty and thus far more in keeping with the values the West purported to be defending against the Nazis.

The charity and self-sacrifice of these nurses, too, was obviously inspired by the example of Jesus and his teachings concerning solicitude for one's afflicted neighbour. The sort of charity exhibited by the Good Samaritan, she pointed out, demanded not only altruism but also a great deal of simple courage: the man beset by robbers had been not only beaten and bruised, but was in a frightening state beside the road. Thus she showed that the sort of charitable impulse which Nietzsche had found so debilitating and emasculating could in fact inspire a courage of a quality which even soldiers liken to that of the S.S. Nor did these qualities require Christian belief to command admiration from peoples of all cultures and value systems. Nevertheless the heroism of the nurses obviously drew its force from an inspiration that was specifically Western—that authentic Christian spirituality which Simone Weil saw as the most precious source of the justice of the allied cause.

The Unity of "Attention"

Even after Christ had "taken possession" of Simone Weil she confessed that, despite the great feeling of love she had experienced, her intelligence still resisted what had taken place: "Yet I still half refused, not my love but my intelligence. For it seemed to me certain, and I still think so today, that one can never wrestle enough with God ... out of pure regard for the truth."[18] And this resistance helps to explain why, even after her religious experience,

17 Though his "warrior" was most often a cultural metaphor rather than a military ideal.
18 Weil, "Spiritual Autobiography," in *Waiting for God*, 36.

she devoted such intellectual energy to demonstrating how her perception of God could be intelligible to individuals lacking either faith or religious feelings. This she was able to do by utilizing certain key ideas which had been central to her way of perceiving things since adolescence—notably her concept of "attention," as well as other insights which had come to her during her political or factory experiences and travels. She did not hit upon Christian scriptures and then make sense of the world through a prism formed by them, so much as explain how the most important lessons she had derived from her experiences had led her to recognize the remarkable truth value of Christ's teachings. All of Simone Weil's religious writings are those of someone who did indeed wrestle with God out of an uncompromising passion for truth, and one result of this wrestling was to produce a set of analyses which make her sense of God quite comprehensible to her most dispassionate and areligious readers.

Simone Weil's doctrine of "attention" served as a link between several aspects of her personality and thought: her ascetic intellectualism, her love for mathematics, her concern for the poor and oppressed, her innovatively focussed politics, and her unusually empathetic sensitivity. We have seen how, from childhood, Weil turned a probing and demanding curiosity from one subject to another with fresh and original results. She eventually isolated this remarkable spiritual and intellectual quality of hers as a central characteristic of her religious perceptions and of her way of communicating with God. It finally became for her a conception which could facilitate her blending of Eastern and Western contemplative traditions:

> ... prayer consists of attention. It is the orientation of all the attention of which the soul is capable toward God. The quality of the attention counts for much. ... Warmth of heart cannot make up for it.
>
> The highest part of the attention only makes contact with God, when prayer is intense and pure enough. [19]

Thus this quality of the spirit became the inspiration not only of her entire system of thought but of her approach to God. In an age when religious belief was often, following upon Marx and Nietzsche, considered to be an opiate and the antithesis of clear reasoning, Simone Weil declared that the very uncompromising nature of her intellectual probity had led her to a sense of God. This gave her a very

19 Weil, "Reflection of the Right Use of School Studies with a View to the Love of God," in *Waiting for God*, 66.

unusual view of many things. After the capacity of "attention to God," or prayer, the next highest human activity—at least potentially—for her seemed to be school studies. And this was because that activity developed this faculty of attention:

> ... school exercises only develop a lower kind of attention. Nevertheless they are extremely effective in increasing the power of attention.
>
> Although people seem to be unaware of it ... the faculty of attention forms the real object ... of studies. Most school tasks have a certain intrinsic interest as well, but such an interest is secondary. All tasks that really call upon the power of attention are interesting for the same reason and to an almost equal degree.[20]

Thus Simone Weil came to the conclusion, drawn from her own experience, that the same faculty which was central to religious contemplation was also the essence of application to studies—and not only the study of theology or philosophy, but all subjects. She also argued, again with remarkable originality, that the development of this precious faculty need not necessarily be accompanied by immediate success in problem solving:

> If we have no aptitude ... for geometry, this does not mean our faculty for attention will not be developed by wrestling with a problem.... On the contrary it is almost an advantage.
>
> It does not matter much whether we succeed in finding a solution ... although it is important to try really hard to do so. Never ... is a genuine effort of the attention wasted. It always has its effect on the spiritual plane and in consequence on the lower one of the intelligence....

But how can a failure in analysis contribute to our spiritual progress? Here she had her own theory:

> If we concentrate our attention on trying to solve a problem of geometry, and if at the end of an hour we are no nearer to doing so than at the beginning, we have nevertheless been making progress each minute ... in another dimension. Without our knowing ... it, this apparently barren effort has brought more light into the soul. The result will one day be discovered in prayer. Moreover, it may very likely be felt in some department of the intelligence in no way connected with mathematics. Perhaps he who made the unsuccessful effort will one day be able to grasp the beauty of a line of Racine more vividly on account of it.[21]

20 Ibid., 66-67.
21 Ibid., 67-68.

Thus Simone Weil maintained—contrary to the assumption of her generation on the subject—that steady concentration on an intellectual problem was somehow tied up with the faculty for religious contemplation in the Western and Eastern traditions. Thus the nature of religious contemplation was not, as many thought, "anti-intellectual" or irrational but, rather, bound up with the experience of intellectual effort. This shaped her attitude toward education: students, she thought, should work without any competitive urge to gain good marks or other school successes, or even with much sensitivity for the different subjects. Rather they should apply themselves equally to all their tasks with the idea that each one will help to form in them the habitual "attention" which was also (the religious person recognized) the substance of prayer.

She insisted that there was an important distinction to be made between "attention" as she understood it and the faculty of application and that the two should not be confused:

> Most often attention is confused with a kind of muscular effort. If one says to one's pupils: "Now you must pay attention," one sees them contracting their brows, holding their breath, stiffening their muscles. If after two minutes they are asked what they have been paying attention to, they cannot reply. They have been concentrating on nothing. They have not been paying attention. They have been contracting their muscles.
>
> Twenty minutes of concentrated, untired attention is infinitely better than three hours of the kind of frowning application that leads us to say with a sense of duty done: "I have worked well."[22]

Simone Weil's distinction between application and attention is also related to her notion of religious contemplation. The capacity to pay or give attention was not just an intellectual virtue for her but a primary *moral* and spiritual quality. Not only did attention open up a direct perception of God for Simone Weil, but lack of attention was bound up, in some mysterious way, with sin and evil. "True attention," for her, was far more difficult to achieve than most people thought, far more difficult than "application." But the capacity for "true concentration" was at the heart of the drama of man struggling between the forces of good and evil in himself:

> There is something in our soul which has a far more violent repugnance for true attention than the flesh has for bodily fatigue. This something is much more closely connected with evil than is the

22 Ibid., 71-72.

flesh. That is why every time that we really concentrate our attention, we destroy the evil in ourselves. If we concentrate with this
intention, a quarter of an hour of attention is better than many good
works.[23]

What a paradox that Simone Weil, who abandoned the comforts
of the intellectual life to search out concrete solutions for the poor and
afflicted, should maintain that fifteen minutes of concentration destroyed more evil than many good works! But for her, true concentration was a very rare quality—like genuine charity—and true attention
shaped the ideal relationship of man with the universe. Concentration, for her, was not only a worthwhile virtue to students in their
limited scholastic tasks, it was an entire orientation of one's being.
This is clear in her description of the faculty:

> Attention consists of suspending our thought, leaving it detached,
> empty, and ready to be penetrated by the object; it means holding in
> our minds, within reach of this thought, but on a lower level and not
> in contact with it, the diverse knowledge we have acquired which
> we are forced to make use of. Our thought should be in relation to all
> particular and already formulated thoughts, as a man on a mountain
> who, as he looks forward, sees below him, without actually looking
> at them, a great many forests and plains. . . . Our thought should be
> empty, waiting, not seeking anything, but ready to receive the
> object in its naked truth. . . .

And, for her, most intellectual errors grew from a lack of this passiv-
ity:

> All wrong translations, all absurdities in geometry problems, all
> clumsiness of style, and all faulty connection of ideas in composi-
> tions and essays, all such things are due to the fact that thought has
> seized upon some idea too hastily, and being thus prematurely
> blocked, is not open to the truth. . . .
> We do not obtain the most precious gifts by going in search of
> them but by waiting for them. Man cannot discover them by his own
> powers, and if he set out to seek for them he will find in their place
> counterfeits of which he will be unable to discern the falsity.[24]

Who but Simone Weil would link sloppiness in the composition of an
essay, or carelessness in solving a geometry problem, or translating a
passage from a foreign language, with one's relationship with God?
Yet this is precisely what she did with her conception of "attention"

23 Ibid., 72.
24 Ibid., 72-73.

over against mere intellectual application. This faculty had little to do with native intellectual ability or aptitude for different subjects. It was even different from the will to master a problem, or compose, with complete absorption. It was rather a spiritual faculty which shaped one's place in the universe. When one applied true attention, even to a subject like geometry, one transcended the worldly dimension: "The solution of a geometry problem does not in itself constitute a precious gift, but . . . it's the image of something precious. Being a little fragment of particular truth, it is a pure image of the unique, eternal, and living truth."[25] Thus, like Descartes, she perceived a link between a sense of intellectual certitude, mathematical truths, and God. This is why, despite her reservations about modern scientific culture, she was able to ascribe so much dignity to science studies and the intellectual way of life. This she was able to do without pretending that intellectuals were better or more spiritual individuals, closer to God, than manual labourers.

One of Simone Weil's remedies for the oppressive conditions of factory work, as we have seen, was the integration of study with factory or agricultural labour. And she thought that it was a great privilege for young people who had a chance to do so to pass their youth developing their power of attention through study. But Weil did not think that studies made for better persons than work in fields or factories. Peasants and workmen were in conditions which allowed them to be near to goodness through poverty, the absence of pressures involved with social status, and through long drawn-out sufferings. Students possessed advantageous conditions for the spiritual life for, as an occupation, she thought, studies were closer to God because "attention" was their very soul.[26] But there was a sort of divine justice in the fact that while a life of scholarship was, a priori, "nearer to God" because of the concentration necessarily bound up with its exercise, in fact the scholars' situation was not ideal because of all the factors—riches, social or status considerations, and possibilities for self-indulgence—which turned students from a pure regard for the truth. It was possible for distracted students to pass through years of study without developing the required capacity in themselves. Factory or agricultural work, by nature so foreign to study and attention, could in fact allow men and women to more approximate the state of concentration than their more culturally privileged brothers and sisters.

25 Ibid., 73.
26 Ibid., 74.

Simone Weil not only described attention as central to the work conditions and spiritual lives of high school students and mathematicians, auto workers and beet farmers, she also saw it as the very key to human social relationships. It was the sort of attitude toward one's neighbour that an authentic religious sensitivity inspired, and the lack of which was at the heart of the most serious of the world's problems:

> Those who are unhappy have no need of anything in this world but people capable of giving them their attention. The capacity to give one's attention to a sufferer is a very rare and difficult thing; it is almost a miracle; it is a miracle. Nearly all those who think they have this capacity do not possess it. Warmth of heart, impulsiveness, pity are not enough.
>
> In the first legend of the Grail, it is said that the Grail (the miraculous vessel that satisfies all hunger by virtue of the consecrated Host) belongs to the first comer who asks the guardian of the vessel, a king three-quarters paralyzed by the most painful wound, "What are you going through?"
>
> The love of our neighbour in all its fullness simply means being able to say to him: "What are you going through?" It is a recognition that the sufferer exists not only as a unit . . . , or a specimen from the social category "unfortunate," but as a man exactly like us. . . . For this reason it is enough . . . to know how to look at him in a certain way.[27]

Of course it was her perception of the inability of men to look at one another in this "certain way" that was behind the radical conclusions Simone Weil drew from her experiences as a manual labourer. Who asked the modern miner, auto worker, or fisherman "What are you going through?" Neither the factory bosses, nor their "experts," nor the trade union leaders, nor even the most perceptive revolutionaries like Trotsky seemed to ask this question. Moreover she was shocked to find that, in modern life, even the workers themselves failed to ask this question of one another. Who, then, asked this question and gave true attention to the unhappy answer of the world? Her examples were, again, Charlie Chaplin and Jesus Christ.

In the end all of the different forms of attention which Simone Weil described—attention to workers, attention to sufferers, attention to academic subjects, attention to languages or literary composition, attention to one's neighbour and to the peculiarities of the modern culture which oppresses him—even attention to God—were tied together. One approached all these different phenomena with basi-

27 Ibid., 75.

cally the same orientation as that with which one looked at the sufferer, the beaten man by the wayside encountered by the Good Samaritan: "this way of looking is first of all attentive. The soul empties itself of all its own contents in order to receive into itself the being it is looking at, just as he is, in all his truth. Only he who is capable of attention can do this."[28] In this way all aspects of Simone Weil's thought reveal themselves to have a certain unity: she was capable of fusing her intellectualism, her love of the Greeks and mathematics, her socialism, and her empathy for Eastern and Western mysticism, into one central and common doctrine. This, she admitted, would necessarily appear paradoxical to many but, for her at least, it all came together just the same:

> So it comes about that, paradoxical as it may seem, a Latin prose or a geometry problem, even though done wrong, may be of great service one day provided we devote the right kind of effort to them. Should the occasion arise, they can one day make us better able to give someone . . . exactly the help required to save him.[29]

The development of the faculty of true attention, then, was the most basic need for ameliorating human life, in individuals and in societies of all ideological persuasions. One need not have religious belief in order to appreciate the value of concentration (in fact Weil herself, as we have seen, appreciated its value long before she had feelings she considered to be religious). Nevertheless the fostering of the capacity for true attention was certainly a central requirement and perhaps the most important benefit of any pure and authentic religion. Thus Weil was able to articulate a concept which in her own life was deeply affected by religious, even mystical experience, but was comprehensible and attractive to non-religious individuals despite its great harmony with some of the most profound religious values of both Western and Eastern traditions. In creating a doctrine which she thought was paradoxical, she was in fact able to resolve painful paradoxes for those who had been troubled by the apparent contradictions between socialist impulses and religious belief, intellectual lucidity and religious sensitivity.

One reason for this resolution of tensions was very simple: for Simone Weil love of God and love of neighbour were made up of the same substance—attention. And since they were of the same substance they were essentially the same love.

28 Ibid., 75.
29 Ibid., 75-76.

The Three Secret Presences of God

Stephen Daedalus[30] found that when the Jesuits in his prep school spoke of God, all he could visualize was "oceans of grey tapioca pudding." When Simone Weil spoke of how to pay attention to, or love, a neighbour it was clear to what she was referring—until she spoke of paying attention to or loving God the father of Jesus. This was another matter: it is not easy to love oceans of grey tapioca pudding. But on this subject, as in so many others of a religious nature, Weil did not—as have so many others who have written on these subjects—simply retreat into pious or mystical language. One need not be a religious believer or disciple of Simone Weil to appreciate her perceptions and arguments in this area. They indicate that even after her "possession by Christ" she did not suspend her demanding intellect in her approach to religious matters. On the contrary, her mystical experience seemed to enlighten and clarify her analyses.

God is really, though secretly, present in only three things on earth, she thought: religious ceremony, the beauty of the world, and our neighbour. In loving these three objects, one implicitly loved God. The combination of these three loves constituted the love of God in the form best suited to the preparatory period, that is to say a veiled form:

> They do not disappear when the love of God in the full sense of the word wells up in the soul; they become infinitely stronger and all loves taken together only make a single love.
>
> The veiled form of love necessarily comes first however, and often reigns alone in the soul for a very long time. Perhaps, with a great many people, it may continue to do so till death. Veiled love can reach a very great degree of purity and power.[31]

One of the most pronounced features of Weil's view of the modern age in the West was its lack of authentic religion: this was a period characterized by religious surrogates such as Nazism or the cult of modern science. Although the West called itself Christian, in fact it was remarkably the contrary:

> Never since the dawn of history, except for a certain period of the Roman Empire, has Christ been so absent as today. The separation of religion from the rest of social life, which seems natural even to the majority of Christians nowadays, would have been judged monstrous by antiquity.[32]

30 In James Joyce, *The Portrait of the Artist as a Young Man* (New York, 1968).
31 Weil, "Forms of the Implicit Love of God," in *Waiting for God*, 96.
32 Weil, "The Love of God and Affliction," in *Weil Reader*, 465.

In the modern age, even the ways of loving God in a veiled form—via religious ceremonies, beauty, and loving one's neighbour—were noticeably lacking. "Real love and respect for religious practices," she found, were "rare even among those who are most assiduous in observing them, and are practically never to be found in others. Most people do not even conceive them to be possible." She thought that a grasp of the supernatural purpose of affliction, compassion, and gratitude, which she had isolated as involved with what was best in the West's spiritual heritage, were not only rare but had become "almost unintelligible for almost everyone today. The very idea of them has almost disappeared; the very meaning of the words has been debased."[33] Thus two of the secret presences of God—in liturgy and love of neighbour—were almost lost to us. This helped explain the lack of a sense of God, the absence of religion, in modern culture.

The secret presence of God remained for modern men in the beauty of the world. Moreover she thought that generally speaking the beauty of the world was the commonest, easiest, and most natural way of approaching a sense of God. But modern Westerners had almost lost all feeling for this—despite the fact that it was "almost the only way by which we allow God to penetrate us." Western imperialism had also seemed bent on making this feeling disappear from "all the continents where they have penetrated with their armies, their trade, and their religion." But despite the relative absence of love for the beauty of creation in the West it remained one of our civilization's last, best hopes:

> ... a sense of beauty, although mutilated, distorted and soiled, remains rooted in the heart of man as a powerful incentive. It is present in all preoccupations of secular life. If it were made true and pure it would sweep all secular life in a body to the feet of God.
> The soul's natural inclination to love beauty is the trap God most frequently uses in order to win it and open it to the breath from on high.[34]

So while a capacity to love the beauty of the world held out hope for the West, this faculty or feeling had to be appreciated for what it was, made more pure and true in order for men to perceive God more directly in the difficult context of the modern age. And in much the same way, Westerners could also hold hope for moral and spiritual renewal in one aspect of their cultural legacy that, paradoxical as it may seem, was "of" their culture but transcended it. Modern Western

33   Weil, "Implicit Love," in *Waiting for God*, 117-18.
34   Ibid.

culture, one of the most corrupt and brutal the world had seen since
the time of the Romans, still held to the legacy of mankind's greatest
teacher, Jesus. Although Christ's teachings were for the most part
rejected or ignored, he still had a precarious presence for the people
he had come to save. He had revealed the very secret of the universe to
debased peoples precisely because they were those in the world most
in need of him.

What was true of the Romans and ancient Hebrews was also
true of modern Westerners, not because they deserved revelation,
but because they *needed* it most. They had been given the most
concise and direct revelation of the nature of reality. This was tied up
with a particular form of comportment that she saw as a supernatural
virtue:

> The supernatural virtue of justice consists of behaving exactly as
> though there were equality when one is stronger in an unequal
> relationship. Exactly, in every respect, including the slightest de-
> tails of accent and attitude.... He who treats as equals those who
> are far below him in strength really makes them a gift of the quality
> of human beings, of which fate has deprived them. As far as it is
> possible for a creature, he reproduces the original generosity of the
> Creator with regard to them.[35]

This quality of empathy and compassion was, of course, central
to the teachings and example of Jesus. But she also saw it as a universal value, indicative of authentic and pure religious inspiration: "This
is the most Christian of virtues. It is also the virtue which the Egyptian
Book of the Dead describes in words sublime as even those of the
Gospel. 'I have never caused anyone to weep. I have never made
anyone afraid. I have never been deaf towards justice and truth.' "[36]
The orientation of these values was, of course, directly inverse to
Nietzsche's "will to power" (as popularly understood), and com-
pletely antithetical to "warrior virtues" from the Romans through the
Nazis.

Granted that an appreciation for Jesus' teachings and a feeling for
the beauty of the world were the two ways in which Western man
could approach God; what, if anything, did these two perceptions
have to do with one another? Here Simone Weil again displayed an
ability to forge a basic unity between two unrelated phenomena: "The
beauty of the world is Christ's tender smile for us coming through
matter. He is really present in universal beauty. The love of this beauty

35 Ibid., 101.
36 Ibid.

proceeds from God dwelling in our souls and goes out to God present in the universe."[37] Of course the Christian tradition had not proven particularly receptive to this conjuncture of sensitivity to beauties and feelings. But she saw this difficulty as tragic, not inevitable. It all tied in with her distinctive view of Western history in which all could have happened differently if Christianity had not been perverted by the Romans and the Roman tradition. In the eleventh and twelfth centuries, particularly in Languedoc, there had been a great hope for a reconciliation of the tragically divergent sets of impulses in the West: some of the troubador compositions of that period, she thought, indicated that if the peculiar sort of Renaissance germinating there had been allowed to develop, ". . . perhaps Christian inspiration and the beauty of the world would not have been separated."[38]

Thus Simone Weil's earlier interest in the civilization of Languedoc proved not so arcane and exotic as it once seemed. The reconciliation between an attachment to Christ's teachings and a love for the beauty of the world seemed almost to have been achieved there—not only in an occasional monastery with its lovely garden, but in an entire culture, among peoples of all social classes and personality orientations. Since she thought that the beauty of the world and Christ's teachings were the two approaches to God most susceptible of touching modern men, she maintained that a revival of the kind of Catharist Christian thought practiced in that time and place was vital for Westerners.

Love for the beauty of the world could be recognized as a cultural universal—albeit existing to greatly varying degrees—at all times and places, in all civilizations and in all periods of history. But what of the approach to life taught by Christ? Was this not, as Nietzsche suggested, a dubious Western invention distinguished by what Nietzsche called an "evil eye for the world"? Simone Weil argued, on the contrary, that her attachment to the person and teachings of Jesus was rooted in the very nature of God, creation, and what she called the "universal revelation" of God to men:

> On God's part creation is not an act of self-expansion but of restraint and renunciation. God and all his creatures are less than God alone. God accepted this dimunition. He emptied a part of His being from Himself. . . . God permitted the existence of things distinct . . . and worth infinitely less than Himself. By this creative act He denied Himself, as Christ has told us to deny ourselves. God

37 Ibid., 120.
38 Ibid., 117.

denied Himself . . . to give us the possibility of denying ourselves
for Him. This response, . . . which it is in our power to refuse, is the
only possible justification for the folly of love of the creative act.[39]

Thus the teachings and sacrificial death of Jesus—which many, from
Christians such as Tertullian through such non-believers as
Nietzsche, have seen as absolutely indefensible before the critical
intellect—made perfect sense to Simone Weil. She worked out a
notion of "decreation," possibly rooted in a minor Jewish theology,[40] which explained the universe in terms of the generosity and
compassion which Christ taught to be the most important human
virtues. For her, the living out of these qualities was not absurd, a
dangerous luxury, or an irrational folly, but found its model in God
himself. As a concrete example she demonstrated how the "decrea-
tive" generosity of the Samaritan in Christ's parable was, paradoxi-
cally, not a self-denial but a creative act—similar to God's in creating
the world:

> Christ taught us that the supernatural love of our neighbour . . .
> happens in a flash between two beings, one possessing and the
> other deprived of human personality. One of the two is only a little
> piece of flesh, naked, inert, and bleeding beside a ditch; he is
> nameless, no one knows anything about him. Those who pass by
> this thing scarcely notice it. . . . Only one stops and turns his atten-
> tion toward it. . . . The attention is creative. But at the moment when
> it is engaged it is a renunciation. . . . The man accepts being di-
> minished by concentrating on an expenditure of energy, which will
> not extend his own power but will only give existence to a being
> other than himself, who will exist independently of him. Still more,
> to desire the existence of the other is to transport himself unto him
> by sympathy, and, as a result, to have a share in the state of inert
> matter which is his.[41]

Simone Weil did not think that a realization that God himself was the
very model for the sort of compassion practiced by the Good Samaritan was a religious insight which was only found among men who
had heard the words of Christ. On the contrary, she thought it was a
universal religious insight found, albeit in greatly varying degrees, in
religions and civilizations at all times and places—much like sensitivity to the beauty of the world. She proposed that this fundamental

39 Ibid., 102.
40 Cf. W. Rabi, "La conception weilienne de la création. Rencontre avec la Kabbale
    juive," in *Simone Weil, Philosophe, historienne et mystique*, 141-154.
41 Weil, "Implicit Love," in *Waiting for God*, 103.

and vital perception be the standard against which all religions be evaluated:

> The religions which have a conception of this renunciation, this voluntary distance, this voluntary effacement of God, His apparent absence and His secret presence here below, these religions are true religion, the translation into different languages of the great Revelation. The religions which represent divinity as commanding wherever it has the power to do so are false. Even though they are monotheistic they are idolatrous.[42]

The great paradox of Western history, then, was that this most aberrant civilization, with its array of religion-substitutes from modern science through Hitlerism, also had been touched by the most eloquent representative of true religion: Jesus Christ. It was consistent in Simone Weil's way of viewing history that this was precisely why Christ had come at the time and place in that same Roman empire which was at the root of so many modern woes. And when he came "all the evil diffused throughout the Roman Empire" was concentrated on him and "it became only suffering to Him." In a mysterious way, she concluded, this transference constitutes the redemption.[43]

Thus the West, that most anti-religious of civilizations, had been given the Redeemer of all mankind and his religious teaching. It was the persistent, terrible rejection of Christ by the West that allowed Simone Weil to be so deeply attached to Christ and yet so critical of "Christian civilization" and open to the religions of other civilizations. Her later studies made her always more deeply attached to Christ, always more sympathetic to non-Christian approaches to the truths which Christ represented and revealed. Thus as a devout Christian she was able to call for an extremely broad-minded approach to the study of comparative religions while yet avoiding religious syncretism and keeping Christ at the centre of all her reflections: "Among the different forms of religion there are . . . hidden equivalents which can only be caught sight of by the most penetrating discernment. Each religion is an original combination of explicit and implicit truths; what is explicit in one is implicit in another."[44] A sense of the "hidden equivalents" between different religions led Simone Weil to argue that one who was born into a religion "not too unsuitable for pronouncing the name of the Lord," and who loved this native religion, would seldom find a legitimate motive for giving it up. Beyond that,

42 Ibid., 102.
43 Ibid., 144.
44 Ibid., 138.

most often, perhaps always, the soul which has reached the highest
realm of spirituality is confirmed in the love of the tradition which
served as it were a ladder."[45] She granted that there were legitimate,
even necessary, reasons for some people to adopt a "foreign religion."
But, despite all of the varieties of religion in the West, she concluded
that "... in principle, directly or indirectly, in a close or distant
manner, it is the Catholic religion which forms the native spiritual
background of all men belonging to the white races."[46] Thus, for better
or for worse, Westerners had a religious tradition that was both Roman
and Christian. That which was "Roman" was what was worst about
the West, that which was truly "Christian" was best.

But behind this set of perceptions Weil had a general theory of the
value of practising religion that she stated concisely and clearly:

> The virtue of religious practices is due to a contact with what is
> perfectly pure, resulting in the destruction of evil.
> ... The church may be ugly, the singing out of tune, the priest
> corrupt and the faithful inattentive. In a sense that is of no impor-
> tance. It is as with a geometrician who draws a figure to illustrate a
> proof. If the lines are not straight and the circles are not round it is of
> no importance. Religious things are pure by right, theoretically,
> hypothetically, by convention. Therefore their purity is uncon-
> ditioned. No stain can sully it.[47]

So Simone Weil concludes that by employing a "true religion"—one's
own, or if need be, a foreign one—as a ladder, one can experience a
transforming love of God.

This transforming love of God was an answer to the savagery of
the Nazis and cruelty of the Soviet Union under Stalin. Such a religious sensitivity was anything but an opiate or distortion for her. On
the contrary she saw it as offering direct and pure contact with
Reality:

> Our neighbour, our friends, religious ceremonies, and the beauty of
> the world do not fall to the level of unrealities after the soul has had
> direct contact with God. On the contrary, it is only then that these
> things become real. Previously these were half dreams. Previously
> there was no reality.[48]

Simone Weil, like Pascal, had brilliant natural gifts for mathematics, literature, languages, and philosophy, but like him, turned her

45 Ibid., 139.
46 Ibid.
47 Ibid., 139-40.
48 Ibid., 168.

vast intellectual powers to religious concerns. Like Pascal she died without having had the time to work out her system of thought, and like his, hers has to be put together from letters, odd essays, and aphorisms. Both wrote, with great precision, to convince sceptics of the value of religion. But both had a love/hate relationship with the Catholic Church that left them on the fringes of heresy. The great difference between Pascal and Simone Weil was in their ultimate grasp of reality. After his great mystical experience of "Fire," of contact with "the God of Abraham, the God of Isaac, the God of Jacob, not of philosophers and scholars," God was reality for Pascal and the external world became even "infinitely silent." He had never had much faith in love or friendship, much feeling for the beauty of the world, or much sensitivity to the value of religious ceremonies; his firsthand contact with God made him withdraw even further from taking these things seriously. Simone Weil always found great meaning in friendship and charity towards the unfortunate, in beauty, and in religious rites. Her sensitivity to those things led her to God and once she thought she had found Him she tried to show others how these things could lead them there too. Her contact with God did not make these important aspects of her life less real but, as she insisted, more real for her. This is one reason why Pascal was "sublime" but rather world-hating and gloomy while Simone Weil, despite the strong ascetic vein in her life and writings and her tragic death, was a rather serene and happy person.

CONCLUSION

Simone Weil's analysis of factory work is illustrative of the strengths and weaknesses in her early political and social thought. Despite the universal applicability of her ideas, her empathy for workers, and the remarkable rapport she was able to establish with them, her views were, at times, distinctly those of a *normalienne*. Several of the horrors of factory work she recorded were particularly painful for a sensitive, highly intelligent and inexperienced product of an unusually doting Parisian upper-middle-class family. Then, too, Simone was more than normally awkward; she was frail and suffered from headaches and self-inflicted under-nourishment. But even if she had been robust and had had a rougher childhood, her lively intelligence would have made most factory work intolerable for her. The dullness and monotony of the assembly line, the impediments to workers solving technical problems associated with their work, were particularly aggravating to individuals with active intellects.

Still, like a good student of Alain, she assumed that a key to alleviating the oppressiveness of factory work would be for the worker to learn for himself the rationale, the intellectual challenge, in his particular task. Was this true for many workers? She admitted that the more intelligent workers seemed more virtuous to her. Could this not lead to serious errors in analysis? And did not this signify a certain involuntary elitism on its own (e.g., would not her efforts to teach mathematics to Breton fishermen lead her to respond more warmly to fishermen of higher intelligence, with a natural aptitude for mathematics)?

Weil's denial of the beneficial effect of technological progress associated with productive labour is surely a major weak point in her

98

analysis. Indeed a sympathetic reader would perhaps portray it as an extreme Luddite view adopted for rhetorical purposes. Few could deny that, from almost every point of view, conditions are now better and easier on the Renault assembly line than they were at the height of the Great Depression. And, then too, the French peasants on the comfortable tractors of the 1980s have easier circumstances than had the beet farmers toiling under the hot sun of Auvergne in the 1940s. For all the nobility and stoic virtues of the pre-war Breton fisherman's life, one could have a more civilized existence on a radar-equipped factoryship than in the old wooden barque.

Simone Weil, however, had always argued for a total vision of the effects of technology on society. It would be fairer to compare the entire "quality of life" of a worker in the thirties with a worker fifty years later to see if the technological advances brought to assembly-line work were not paid for heavily in some other area of life. How did the total environment—food, housing, leisure time activities, the feeling of community, a sense of meaning in work—of the Renault worker in her day compare with that of the men of Boulogne-Billancourt and Detroit today? On second look, this is not so easy to answer. Should we compare rates of alcoholism, of divorce, of stress, of suicide? Who could say with any assurance after the great post-war studies of the effect of stress, noise, and other environmental pollution, junk foods, and technological advances on the entire human environment that things are certainly better for factory workers now than in her day? She called for a broadly focussed attention to the lot of workers, and that is not achieved more easily—or more often—today than back then.

The great significance of Weil's early analyses of factory work and political and social issues comes from its originality of focus. Decades later, how many intellectuals who speak with authority about the proletariat are working alongside their subjects on assembly lines, farms, or boats?[1] And how many studies have the range and perception which Simone Weil brought to hers?

Simone Weil's analysis of the influence of the Roman Empire on the West also remains provocative and interesting. Westerners have become far less confident in the righteousness of their imperialistic initiatives than they were forty years ago. The condemnations of Western imperialisms and revolts against the European imperial

1 Recently the author posed this question to experts discussing the working class in Europe. It elicited a rather embarrassed response. Cf. the session in "Classes Under Socialism" in the proceedings of the Colloquium The Future of Socialism in Europe (Interuniversity Centre for European Studies, Montreal) (forthcoming).

powers since World War II have made her attack upon the origins of the imperial impulse in the West seem ever more perceptive over the years. But the violence of her polemic, her failure to mention the more positive aspects of Roman civilization, force us to admit that her description of Rome and the Roman tradition was somewhat distorted by her passionate rhetoric. Certainly, Western society owes more to Roman law and political organization, to Virgil, Marcus Aurelius, or Tacitus, than she implied.

If Weil's treatment of the Romans was sometimes distorted, her descriptions of the history of the Jews was even more so. In contrast to her vast knowledge of Greek literature and civilization, and her study of Sanskrit to better absorb the culture of India, her knowledge of Judaism was relatively superficial and hastily acquired: she had no direct experience of Jewish culture and religion in her family, never evinced an interest in learning Hebrew, and seemed to base her entire understanding of the Hebrews on her reading of the Old Testament. Thus Weil gave no indication of having read the Talmud or of having any familiarity with post-biblical rabbinical thought (and this helps explain some of her more questionable historical generalizations in this area—such as her insistence on the decisive, positive, foreign influence on the Hebrews during the Babylonian exile—which seem, today, so difficult to defend). And despite her wide ranging interest in mystical theology, she betrays—apart from, possibly, her own notion of "decreation," the origins of which are unknown—no knowledge of cabala literature, or of contemporary Jewish mystical currents such as the Hassidic. This led her to stress the contrast between the spirituality of the early Hebrews and later Hebrews, and between the Old Testament and the New, to exaggerated lengths.

While Simone Weil's critique of the Romans and the Hebrews has been attacked as highly impressionistic historical interpretation, her unbounded admiration for the Cathars has met with the same sort of criticism. Just like her exaggerations of the brutality and racism of the Romans and Hebrews, some of her eulogies of the Cathars soared far beyond any identifiable documentation. Most historical scholarship on the Cathars would temper Weil's romantic description of a people of saints, even if some modern scholars would support her general interpretation.[2]

2 In 1942 in occupied France, P. Belperron published *La Croisade Contre les Al-bigeois, et l'Union du Languedoc à la France (1209-1249)* (Paris, 1942), *a large and detailed work slanted in favour of the northern invaders of Albigensian territories and thus totally opposed to the interpretation of Simone Weil. In 1961 Jacques Madaule, a veteran member of the* Esprit *group, published* Le Drame Albigeois et le

Simone Weil's admirers regret some of the hyperbole in her discussion of the Romans, Jews, and Cathars—and some of her extremist attitudes regarding the human body and physical love. Contempt for her appearance is one of Weil's most striking characteristics. Her friend Simone Pétrement has described her frequent rejections of physical affection as background to the aphorisms juxtaposing true love to possession, spiritual to physical love. Her admirer Gustave Thibon was shocked by her contempt for comfort, her extraordinarily harsh treatment of her own body.

Some have seen her early death as the culmination of her irrational, even fanatical, contempt for her own flesh. But whatever her personal comportment, several of Weil's aphorisms do not seem particularly healthy or balanced to post-Freudians.

Weil's attitude toward the human body seems tied up with a theological notion—"decreation"—which is no less exotic or remote from contemporary religious thinking. But her theory has found serious scholarly expositors and defenders.[3] The notion of God diminishing himself in creating the universe offers a fresh and, for some, persuasive explanation of the place of Christ's sacrifice on the cross. The notion of God's "retreat" from the world, of Christ's deference to the lawfulness of creation, can offer solace to individuals (such as Albert Camus) haunted by the metaphysical implications of the sufferings of innocent people. If self-abnegation and suffering and the "obedience" of creation are the very meaning of the universe, then neither the agony of Jesus nor the pain of an innocent child are absurd and incomprehensible.

The notion of decreation can be useful in reconciling the existence of the most terrible human agonies with the existence of a good God. But it is less easy to reconcile with certain other aspects of Christian belief and tradition. Christ's voluntary self-sacrifice might be more comprehensible in such a perspective, but his announcement of the kingdom is less so. The whole messianic tradition in Judaism,

Destin Français (Paris, 1961) which had much the same theme. Almost contemporaneously Zoe Oldenbourg published her *Massacre at Montsegur* (London, 1961), a vivid popular history favourable to both the southerners and heretics and, of course, the general conception of Simone Weil. The villains are the church and Simon de Montfort, and her exhaustive research is only marred by a strong bias in favour of the Cathars, similar to Weil's. P. Wolff's editing of a *Histoire du Languedoc* (Toulouse, 1967) and R. Belli's *Histoire du Languedoc* (Paris, 1974) have both furthered Languedocian scholarship. Belli is a neo-Cathar and his preoccupation with the religious and cultural heritage of the Midi shows that Weil's ideas cannot be dismissed out of hand.

3 Cf. Miklos Vëto, *La métaphysique religieuse de Simone Weil* (Paris, 1971).

taken over and transformed by Christ, is difficult to reconcile with the world view of Simone Weil. As an extreme platonist, she tended to emphasize the role of Christ as the Word of divine wisdom, the teacher of the secret of eternal life. She largely ignored Jesus' role in human history, and that of the church. Her critical attitude toward Judeo-Christian tradition and its most sacred institutions entailed an extreme insensitivity to centuries of efforts by Jews and Christians on behalf of the poor and oppressed. She had little to say on the social and political philosophy of the Catholic Church, on the papal "social" encyclicals, or about the saints who approximated her ideals. Even Christian history, for her, was "a tissue of base and cruel acts."

In sum, most of the difficulties in the thought of Simone Weil came from the exaggerations in her positions. Critics might well agree that the Romans or the early Hebrews had brutal qualities, but reject her totally sombre portrait of their influence on history. Some might agree that the Albigensians were more noble than their enemies, or that spiritual love is as important as physical, but reject her more extravagant generalizations on these subjects.

While Simone Weil's tendency to rhetorical simplification may have undermined some of her historical arguments, these same qualities helped to foster her originality. Her youthful insistence on putting acts in accord with ideas led her to share the lot of farm and factory labourers, and produce a brilliant portrait of the proletarian condition. Her determination to know the worker's life first-hand, fool-hardy to her fellow *normaliens*, inspired her admirers . . . and yet today can stimulate fresh attitudes toward the work place.

Just as Weil's "exaggerated" determination to share the lot of the poor produced some remarkable insights into oppression in industrial societies, so too her total opposition to all forms of brutality, to all aggressive nationalisms and racisms, helped her to assume an unusual prophetess role among her fellow Gaullists in London. Her opposition to the imperialistic and nationalist currents in the West forced her readers to re-examine the place of these phenomena within the Judeo-Christian tradition.

In her total rejection of the psychological notion of "sublimation," too, Simone Weil encouraged a rethinking of the place of the spiritual dimensions in human relationships. Again, her powerful, uncompromising, critical intelligence forced the re-examination of old clichés. Here again her rejection of modern *mores* challenges basic assumptions of our culture and rationalizations of our comportment.

Simone Weil's notion of love was as outside of contemporary norms as her religiosity was out of the ordinary. Her perceptions were Jesus-centred and seemed to have little to do with modern Catholic, Protestant, or Jewish theology. In fact, her focus on Jesus and his sayings, her doctrine of attention, had little to do with any form of theological speculation. While Simone Weil may have produced an original, sophisticated, and impressive "religious metaphysics" of her own, her religiosity was largely founded on simple parables of Jesus, particularly that of the Good Samaritan. Weil's religious energies seemed largely focussed on developing "attention" to the poor and oppressed. This made most contemporary theology irrelevant.

Simone Weil's centring of her life around an attention to the afflicted, inspired by Jesus, made her an ecumenist. Differences of theology and ritual meant less than attention to God and to one's neighbour, and, like Mother Teresa of Calcutta, the more she came to respect the spiritual values of India, the more her devotion to Jesus deepened. Weil's comments on oriental spirituality have recently been seriously studied by scholars.[4] Just as the religious style of Mother Teresa inspires Christians and non-Christians, Westerners and Easterners, so too Weil's thought can be of special interest to non-Westerners interested in spirituality. In fact, her spiritual genius seems particularly noticeable to non-Westerners and to non-believers.[5]

Simone Weil's importance lies in her unique religious perceptions, that remarkable sense of God which set her off from the rest of her generation. Her sensitivity to the "secret presence" of God, and her notion of "attention," can be seen as within the neo-Platonic tradition. Nevertheless Simone Weil remains one of the most imaginative and original spiritual writers of our century.

4 Especially David Raper.
5 E.g., Simone Pétrement has been facilitating the translating of the complete works of Simone Weil into Japanese.

APPENDIX

The "New York Notebook" (1942)

The following selected aphorisms are from Simone Weil's "New York Notebook" in which she recorded her thoughts not long before her death. They are reprinted by permission from Simone Weil, First and Last Notebooks, translated by Richard Rees (London: Oxford University Press, 1970), pages 82, 84, 97, 112, 138-139, 140, 176, 182, 198-199, 208, 210, 216-217-218, 229-230, 249, 254-255, 275, 287-288.

♦ ♦ ♦ ♦ ♦

Man is like a castaway, clinging to a spar and tossed by the waves. He has no control over the movement imposed on him by the water. From the highest heaven God throws a rope. The man either grasps it or not. If he does, he is still subject to the pressures imposed by the sea, but these pressures are combined with the new mechanical factor of the rope, so that the mechanical relations between the man and the sea have changed. His hands bleed from the pressure of the rope, and he is sometimes so buffeted by the sea that he lets go, and then catches it again.

But if he voluntarily pushes it away, God withdraws it.

♦ ♦ ♦ ♦ ♦

One of the most exquisite pleasures of human love—to serve the loved one without his knowing it—is only possible, as regards the love of God, through atheism.

♦ ♦ ♦ ♦ ♦

Every movement of pure compassion in a soul is a new descent of Christ upon earth to be crucified.

♦ ♦ ♦ ♦ ♦

God must be impersonal, to be innocent of evil, and personal, to be responsible for good.

♦ ♦ ♦ ♦ ♦

Scientists believe in science in the same way that the majority of Catholics believe in the Church, namely, as Truth crystallized in an infallible collective opinion; they contrive to believe this in spite of the continual changes of theory. In both cases it is through lack of faith in God.

♦ ♦ ♦ ♦ ♦

Truly beautiful human beings deserve to be loved. But the concupiscence inspired by the beauty of a face and a body is not the love that this beauty deserves; it is a sort of hate which grips the flesh when it confronts something which is too pure for it. Plato knew that.

♦ ♦ ♦ ♦ ♦

We are abandoned in time.
God is not in time.

♦ ♦ ♦ ♦ ♦

Joy fixes us to eternity and pain fixes us to time. But desire and fear hold us in bondage to time, and detachment breaks the bonds.

♦ ♦ ♦ ♦ ♦

The purpose of human life is to construct an architecture in the soul.

♦ ♦ ♦ ♦ ♦

Humility is the root of all authentic virtues. Chastity, for example. Temperance. Patience.

♦ ♦ ♦ ♦ ♦

For Protestants, who no longer have the Church, religion has become to a great extent national. Hence the revived importance of the Old Testament.

♦ ♦ ♦ ♦ ♦

Anyone who, at the moment when he is thinking of God, has not renounced everything, without exception, is giving the name of God to one of his idols.

◆ ◆ ◆ ◆ ◆

Creation is a fiction of God's.

◆ ◆ ◆ ◆ ◆

The beauty of the world has almost disappeared from Christianity, because the Roman Empire turned it into a political religion.

◆ ◆ ◆ ◆ ◆

And when we speak of "burning" with love, the word must come from the tradition of seeing the wood burning for love of us, to give us warmth and light.

The Sun, the Father. The wood, Christ. The light, the Spirit. The sun gives the light to the tree and the tree gives it to men.

◆ ◆ ◆ ◆ ◆

But the Roman Empire was never really destroyed. It is what still afflicts the world. Its contamination of Christianity was so profound that Christianity became its means of survival.

◆ ◆ ◆ ◆ ◆

The thought of death gives a colour of eternity to the events of life. If we were granted everlasting life in this world, our earthly life, by gaining perpetuity, would lose that eternity whose light shines through it.

◆ ◆ ◆ ◆ ◆

One can project sexuality upon any kind of object; collector's hobby, money, power, group membership, cat, canary, God (but in this case it won't be the true God).

Or one can kill sexuality and effect a transmutation of the energy it contained.

This operation is what detachment is.

Every attachment is of the same nature as sexuality. In that, Freud is right (but only in that).

God has deposited in us a supplementary energy. It is the talent in the parable. Some exploit it themselves automatically, to the accompaniment of sensual pleasure. Others give it as food to the better part of their soul.

◆ ◆ ◆ ◆ ◆

... as a parasite lays its eggs in an animal's flesh, God places a sperm in our soul which, when it has grown, will be his Son. . . . Our soul ought to be nothing except a place of welcome and nourishment for this divine germ. We ought not to give food to our soul. We ought to give our soul as food for this germ. After which it will itself obtain direct nourishment from everything that formerly nourished our soul. Our soul is the egg within which this divine germ grows to a bird. As an embryo, the bird feeds on the egg; once it has grown it breaks the shell and emerges and pecks for grain. Our soul is shut off from all reality by an enclosing skin of egoism, subjectivity, and illusion; the germ of Christ, placed in our soul by God, feeds on this; when it has grown enough it breaks the soul, explodes it, and makes contact with reality. That is Love in the microcosm. Love in the macrocosm, when once its golden wings have grown, breaks the egg of the world and passes to the place beyond the sky.

INDEX

Abelard, Peter, 66
Action Française, 37
affliction, 75, 91
"Alain" (Emile-Auguste Chartier), 2, 4, 8-11, 24, 32, 65, 77, 98
Albigensianism, Albigensians, 54, 65-73, 93, 100-102
Amalekites, 48, 73
anarchism, 2, 18
anthropology, 58
Aragon, Louis, 7
Aron, Raymond, 1
Astarte, 50
atheism, 53, 56, 62, 71-72, 104
"Attention," 19, 82-97, 103
Audry, Colette, 12-13, 15

Baal, 50
Baptism (Sacrament of), 78
Barrès, Maurice, 37-38
beauty, 91, 93-94, 106
Beauvoir, Simone de, 7-16, 19
Belli, R., 101
Belperron, P., 100n.
Bernanos, Georges, 1, 37, 43-44
Bhagavat-Gita, 79-80
Bloy, Léon, 37
Book of the Dead, 92
Bossuet, 51
bourgeoisie, 7-11, 19

Brasillach, Robert, 7
British Empire, 56
Bugnion-Secretan, P., 4n.

C.G.T. (Confédération Générale du Travail), 34
cabala, 100
cadres (bureaucratic elites), 21-23, 25, 34-35, 88
Caesar, Julius, 57
Cameron, J. M., 4
Camus, Albert, 1, 3, 5, 17, 72, 101
capitalism, 18, 21-23, 26, 35
Cathars, Catharism, 5, 51-52, 54, 65-73, 93, 100-101
Caute, David, 19n.
Chaldeans, 49
Chaplin, Charlie, 36, 77, 88
charity, 86
chastity, 70, 105
China, 49, 61
Christ, Jesus, 5, 36, 38-39, 45-46, 48-50, 55, 60-61, 63-64, 69-72, 74-80, 82-83, 88, 90, 92-95, 101-103, 105
Christianity, 3, 5, 51, 53-55, 70, 72, 74-75, 95, 106
Church, Roman Catholic, 3, 16, 51, 58, 64, 69, 71, 73, 96-97, 105
Cicero, 57

Claudel, Paul, 37
Clement, Dom, 80
Communism, Communist Party, 7, 12, 18-19, 21-22, 25-34, 43
Communist Manifesto (1848), 25-26
Crozier, Michel, 22

Daedalus, Stephen, 90
Daniel, 48
Daniélou, Cardinal Jean, S.J., 5
Davy, Marie-Magdeleine, 4n.
death, 106
Debidour, Victor-Henri, 4n.
decreation, 93-94, 101
democracy, 26-27
Descartes, René, 24-25, 87
Dionysus, 62, 78
Drieu la Rochelle, Pierre, 7
druids, 57
Dujardin, Philippe, 4n., 10, 17
Durruti, 43

Egypt, religious traditions of, 49, 54, 62, 66, 92
Elijah, 48
Eliot, T. S., 57-58
Ellul, Jacques, 22-23, 77, 79
energy (sources of), 28-29
Engels, Friedrich, 20, 25
enlightenment, 71
eroticism, 68
Esprit (the review), 79, 100
evil, 85-86, 96

Factory Journal, 33
factory work, 18, 20, 22-23, 27, 29-36, 74, 87, 98, 102
fascism, 7, 19, 21-23, 26, 40-43, 46, 48, 72, 77, 82
Fascism (Italian), 18, 40
February 6, 1934 (riots of), 18
Feuerbach, Ludwig, 25
fishing, fishermen, 31
Fraisse, Simone, 58
Franco, Françisco, 18
Free French, 55, 73, 102
French Revolution, 51
Freud, Sigmund, 106

Gaul, Ancient, 56-57, 62
Gaulle, Charles de, 35, 38, 80
geometry, 86-87, 89, 96
Germany (Nazi), 22, 39-40, 41, 43-46, 52, 56, 64-65, 70, 77, 80, 90, 92, 96
Giniewski, Paul, 4n.
gnosticism, 51, 54, 66
Good Samaritan, 89, 94, 103
Grail (legend), 88
Great Beast, 52-55
Greece (Ancient), 49, 54, 58, 61, 65-66, 70, 78-79, 89
Gregorian Chant, 66, 75
Grenier, Richard, 38n.
Guérin, Bernard, 4n.
Gustave Thibon (Simone Weil's), 75-76, 98
Hebblethwaite, Peter, 1n.
Hegelians, Young, 25, 28
heroism, 41
Hitlerism, 26, 41-46, 53, 55-56, 62, 72, 80-82, 95
Hindu (religious teachings), 70, 79
history, 47-73
Hitler, Adolf, 44-46, 56, 62, 71, 81
"Holocaust," 73
Hughes, H. Stuart, 18

Iliad, the 78
India (religions of), 55, 60-61, 79-80, 100
Inquisition, 67
intellectuals, 35
Isaiah, 48
Israel, the Hebrews, 4, 40, 46, 47-55, 72-73, 80, 100-101

Jansenists, 51
Jesuits, 51, 90
Job, 48
Jouvenel, Bertrand de, 1
Judaism, Jewish tradition, 2, 77, 100-103

Kahn, Gilbert, 5n., 58n.
Kempfner, Gaston, 4n.

Levi-Strauss, Claude, 58
Liberation, 55
Livy, 60
London (Simone Weil in), 55
Louis XIV, 41, 51
Luxemburg, Rosa, 12, 23

Madaule, Jacques, 100-101n.
Malraux, André, 7
Manichaeans, 54, 68
Marc, Alexandre, 77
Marcion, 51, 80
Marcus Aurelius, 100
Marcuse, Herbert, 23
Maritain, Jacques, 37, 63
Maritain, Raïssa, 77
Martinet, Marcel, 23
Marx, Karl, 3, 12, 22-33, 36, 83
Marxism, 3, 18-19, 22-33, 40n., 75-76
Mary, the Virgin, 50
materialism, 53
Maurras, Charles, 37-38, 49
mine work, 20-22, 24, 27-28, 33
Moeller, Charles, 4n.
Montfort, Simon de, 66, 69, 101
Mother Teresa, 103
Mounier, Emmanuel, 1, 79
mysticism, Hassidic, 100
mystics, Mystical Tradition, 63-64, 72, 76, 78, 89, 97

Napoleon, 45, 51
nationalism, 37-43, 45-46, 48, 50, 77, 82, 102
Need for Roots, 3
Neo-platonism, 51, 65
Nietzsche, Friedrich, 47, 49-52, 54, 58, 63, 72, 75, 82-83, 92-94
Nizan, Paul, 7, 12, 15
Nouvelle Héloise, 67
Nurses Corps (Project), 80-82

O'Brien, Conor Cruise, 4
Old Testament, 3, 47-53, 78, 100, 105
Oldenburg, Zoe, 101n.
oppression, 29-33
orthodoxy (Catholic), 67, 80
Osiris, 78

pacifism, 26
Pascal, Blaise, 1, 51, 60, 96-97
patriotism, 37-43, 45-46, 53, 56-57, 82
patristic literature, 54-55, 79
Paul VI, Pope, 1
Péguy, Charles, 38, 79
Perrin, Father J. M., 3, 4n., 5, 37, 54-55, 74, 79-80
Persians, Persia, 49, 54, 66
Pétrement, Simone, 4n., 10-11, 65, 101, 103n.
Peyre, Henri, 5
Pharaoh, 61
"Plan" (of the C.G.T.), 34
Plato, 50, 54, 70, 78, 102, 105
Politzer, Georges, 12
Popper, Karl, 44n.
productivity, 28-30, 32
progress, 26-29, 35-36, 59-60, 64-65, 98-99
Prophets, 52
Protestants, 51, 105
Providence (Divine), 61
Pythagoreans, 66, 69-70

Rabi, Wladimir, 5
Racine, 84
racism, 50, 73, 80, 82, 102
Raper, David, 2, 103n.
Real del Sarte, Maxime, 37
Redemption, Christian doctrine of, 59
Rees, Sir Richard, 4n.
Reformation, Protestant, 51
Renaissance, 51-52, 70
Resistance, French, 3, 38, 40-43, 55
Révolution prolétarienne, 21, 77
Richelieu, 41
Roché, Déodat, 50, 52, 54, 71
Romanesque, 66
Romans, 40, 44, 46, 48, 51-65, 71, 78-79, 90, 92-93, 95, 100-102, 106
Romeo and Juliet, 67
Rougemont, Denis de, 67-70
Rousseau, Jean-Jacques, 51, 67

Saint Bernard of Clairvaux, 66-67
Saint Francis of Assisi, 75

Index

Saint Irenaeus, 55
Saint Joan of Arc, 37, 39
Saint John of the Cross, 80
Saint Paul, 59, 75, 79
Saints (Christian), 60
Sanskrit, 58
Sartre, Jean-Paul, 1, 9, 11-16, 19
Saul, 48, 73
Schumann, Maurice, 4n., 73, 77
science, 22-26, 30, 32, 35, 72, 87, 90, 95, 105
science, history of, 32
slavery, slaves, 34-35, 53, 61-63, 74-75
Socialism, 26, 35, 89
Socrates, 50
Solesmes, Benedictine Abbey of, 75-76
Solzhenitsyn, Alexander, 35
Song of Songs, 48
Souvarine, Boris, 23
Soviet Union, 21-22, 25-26, 31, 43, 76, 96
Spanish Civil War, 13, 18, 43
Spanish Empire, 56
Spanish Republic, 18
Spiritual Autobiography, 74-77
SS (Shutzstaffel), 80-82
Stalin, Stalinism, 21, 23, 40, 43, 46, 48, 71, 77, 96
Stoics, 51, 66
studies (school), 84-89
sublimation, 70
Sulla, 44-45

Tacitus, 100
Talmud, 100
technology, 24-26, 99
Teilhard de Chardin, Pierre, 64
Tertullian, 51, 94
Thibon, Gustave, 4n., 37, 101
Thrace (religion of), 54, 66
Tomlin, G. W. F., 4n.
totalitarianism, 71, 73
trade unions (syndicalism), 3, 18, 34, 66, 75, 77
Tristan and Isolde, 67
Trotsky, Léon, 23-24, 33, 36, 76-77
Trotskyist movement, 2, 12, 21, 23
Troubadours (twelfth century), 54, 66-68

United States, 22, 39

Vëto, Miklos, 101n.
Vichy (Regime), 38-39, 65
Vidal, Canon, 80
Virgil, 57, 100
virginity, 70

Wagner, Richard, 67
Weil, André, 10, 24n., 77
Wolff, Philippe, 101 n.
working class, 30-31, 33-36, 43, 87-88, 98-99
Wisdom, Books of, 52